EMERGENCE FOR LIFE
NOT FALL FROM GRACE

*Making sense of the Jesus story
in the light of evolution*

KEVIN TRESTON

MOSAIC PRESS

Published in Australia by
Mosaic Press
508 High St
Preston Vic. 3072
Australia

Mosaic Press is an imprint of Mosaic Resources Pty Ltd

ISBN 9781743240434

Unless otherwise noted, Scripture quotations are taken from the *New Revised Standard Version Bible*, copyright 1989, Division of Christian Education of the National Council of the Churches of Christ in the United States of America. Used by permission. All rights reserved.

First published 2013

Cataloguing-in-Publication entry is available for the National Library of Australia http:/catalogue.nla.gov.au/.

Book design by John Healy

Printed and bound in Great Britain by
Marston Book Services Limited, Oxfordshire

CONTENTS

INTRODUCTION

One of the greatest challenges for religions today is to remain faithful to the core of their revelation and yet be credible in how their beliefs are communicated in a world shaped by science. The universe is about 13.7 billion years old and the human species, in some primal identity, perhaps one million years old.

The first three chapters of the book of Genesis express in symbolic language the creation of the world, the first humans, creatures and the reality of sinful behaviour. The sacred origin myth describes the goodness of creation and an act of disobedience by Adam and Eve. This act of disobedience was consequently theologically designated as the "Fall". After the fifth century the doctrine of original sin emanated out of the Fall myth and became part of the Christian tradition as an explanation of inherited evil within each person.

However, in the light of the general consensus of scientific opinion about the evolution of the human species, there are almost insuperable scientific obstacles to the veracity of the whole notion of the Fall and the doctrine of original sin, particularly in the literalist mode by which the doctrine has been explained and taught as official Christian teaching. The traditional interpretation of the Fall origin myth and the original sin doctrine have significantly shaped the way the Christ story has been told in Christian theology and worship.

The problem of evil is an ongoing mystery. Every religious tradition recounts myths to explain its presence in the world. The shocking mayhem of World Wars, Holocaust, nuclear weaponry and mass ethnic killings have almost paralysed religious writers in seeking to reconcile the scope of evil in the world with beliefs about a loving God. Faced with suffering, loss and destruction, people cry out in anguish, 'Why would God ever allow this evil to happen?'

The Fall/redemption will always be an enduring historical feature of the traditional Christian story. Much of church teachings, theology, liturgy and devotions are experienced within the framework of the Fall/redemption tradition.

However, is there an alternate interpretation to the Genesis myth as a Fall? Is there an interpretation of the origin myth which is more attuned to what science is saying about evolution, especially the evolution of the human species and consciousness? A rising tide of theological voices are generating questions in the light of evolutionary science about whether the framework of the Fall is a viable context within contemporary consciousness for an interpretation of the mission of Jesus who became the Christ.

One of the most extraordinary features of our contemporary Western culture is the dramatic leap in consciousness in a relatively short space of time. Consciousness opens us out to a larger sphere of understanding and deeper meaning. Something new is happening culturally and it is happening very rapidly. Just think how much cultural thinking has changed even within the last few decades on such matters as the internet, communications technology, globalisation, status of women, ecological concerns, climate change, religious cooperation, genetics, multiculturalism and a hundred other examples we could propose to illustrate the rapidity of radical change. How well does the Christian narrative engage with an evolutionary understanding of the human species and creation?

This book focuses on those Christians whose life and faith are shaped by Western consciousness. Certain assumptions about life and faith in Western orientated countries are not necessarily relevant to Christians in such countries as China, Egypt or indigenous peoples. However, I would hold that many of the basic themes of the book have some application to all Christians in the world.

Science is challenging traditional religions to reframe their messages in accord with scientifically demonstrated evidence. To avoid aligning certain tenets in religious belief with established science is to strain the credibility of believers and non-believers alike. The images and symbols associated with God arise out of the Judeo-Christian tradition in a pre-scientific era. If understood literally, these symbols are increasingly at variance with modern science, especially with an understanding of the evolutionary nature of all things.

It is almost banal to state that Christianity in Western countries is in crisis. The reasons for the decline of Christianity as a vibrant public voice are too complex to analyse in this book. However, one aspect of the crisis in Christianity is the question as to how well the Christian message interacts and transforms cultural consciousness. The Christian community cannot do its mission effectively unless its voice speaks to the lived reality of the people. Another feature of the nature of the crisis is a challenge for religions to transform their mode of communicating beliefs from a literalist to a symbolic mode of expressing their beliefs.

From the perspective of evolutionary science, this book considers an interpretation of the Genesis origin myth as a sacred story of the Emergence of human consciousness on the great journey of enlightenment and not exclusively interpreted as a Fall from a graced life. The evolutionary journey of the human species is told within the overarching evolutionary story of the universe.

The theme of Emergence is explored at two complementary levels. At one level is the evolutionary emergence of human consciousness and cultural change. At another level there is the growing interest in the science of Emergence where new modes of being that are fundamentally different from what has come before come into existence. New, unpredictable properties emerge from other elements which are at a lower level of existence. The science of Emergence has far reaching implications for how a new paradigm of the Christ story might be composed.

In the book there are many references to scientific information. Rather than expound on a diversity of scientific theories, I have chosen those findings distilled from a general consensus of scientific evidence.

The inspiration for the book arose from my own thinking and research on reconciling the traditional literal interpretation of the Genesis origin myth and its subsequent context on the Christian story with the findings of modern evolutionary science. The very idea of God punishing all humankind for all time because of a purported primal moral failing by Adam and Eve simply beggars belief. Likewise, there is surely a problem with the belief that each child is born into a state of original sin instead of beliefs about a child born into a world that is characterised by what is both beautiful and morally flawed.

An added motivation for me in composing this book was reflections on the pastoral experiences of people involved in the communication of the Christian story. Those teaching theology, religious education teachers in schools and colleges, RCIA catechists and people in adult life and faith education groups struggle to communicate the teachings that are specified in the *Catechism of the Catholic Church* about the Fall myth, original sin and the nature of Christ's redemptive mission. The literalism of the official interpretation of the Genesis myth is at variance with the insights of evolutionary science. Any religion must be faithful in its pursuit of truth; otherwise it lacks credibility in communicating its message.

A basic contention in the book is that Christianity, with its core belief in the incarnation, must take evolution seriously and communicate its beliefs within an evolutionary framework. Evolution is perhaps the most important scientific movement in the last 150 years.

My special interest during over fifty years of ministry in many countries is for practical rather than academic theology. My abiding concern in theology is: how does the Christian story impact on the life journeys of people and the wellbeing of creation? Do the origin stories make sense within scientific consciousness and is the Christ story transformational? The problem is not with the Genesis myth itself but with the traditional literal interpretations of the myth. During the composition of this book, I have watched several TV programs on the evolution of the human species. While watching the programs on the various theories about the evolution of the human species, I found myself musing on such questions as:

I wonder what thoughtful Christians would make of this exposition of the various strands of the human species, some of which became extinct or other strands which merged to constitute the modern human species?

What does the evolutionary story of the human species mean in the light of Christian beliefs about the Adam and Eve and the Fall story?

Can a scientific understanding of the evolution of the human species be reconciled with Christian traditional teachings, especially teachings on the mission of Christ?

The book is not directed at professional theologians who have access to a plethora of resources on this topic but rather to Christians at the grassroots levels. The theme of the book is not new and has been discussed for centuries. However, I believe that it is facile to maintain that the topic is exhausted. My pastoral experience suggests that the literalism of the Adam and Eve Fall story and the literalism generally in how dogma are communicated are still firmly entrenched in the lives of ordinary Christians. The many references in the liturgy to the Fall tradition and Christ rectifying the consequences of the Fall attest to its enduring presence in Christian worship and theology.

What is quite disturbing for Catholics is that the *Catechism of the Catholic Church* simply ignores the issue and seems oblivious to the findings of modern evolutionary science in its teachings on the Genesis myth. The word 'evolution' does not appear in the 803 pages of the *Catechism of the Catholic Church*. To understand the reluctance of the official church to engage in the challenges of evolution to its teachings, one needs to appreciate the daunting enterprise of developing a new theological paradigm. An alternative interpretation to the myth as a Fall from grace to an interpretation of Emergence of the human species would open a veritable Pandora's box of theological issues, especially those relating to Christology (a study of Jesus as Christ). However, the option of holding the line on traditional teachings about the Fall is less and less tenable within contemporary scientific consciousness.

Three authors have been very significant in influencing my own thinking on this topic. The works of Adrian Smith (d 2011), Thomas Berry (d 2010) and a recent work by Jack Mahoney SJ have enriched my understanding of Christianity and evolution. After I had completed the first draft of the text, I became aware of *Christianity in evolution* by Mahoney. I would highly recommend this work for those who wish to further pursue the themes of this book. The resources listed in my book point to the growing interest in this topic and have been invaluable to me in composing the text.

I wish to thank the following people for their support, critique and wisdom: Ross and Liz Keane, James and Bernadette Stewart, John Coles, Mary Coloe PBVM, Gerard Hall SM, Patrick Oliver, Bet Green, Catherine Foley, Paula Egan, Helen Treston, Laraine Roberts, Yuri Koszarycz, John Brady, Peter Butler and Garry Everett.

I also wish to express my special gratitude to Mosaic Press who published the book and edited the text. In particular, I would like to thank Hugh McGinlay of Mosaic Press for his encouragement and insightful comments. I also thank John Healy who designed the cover of the book, depicting the image of the tree, the Tree of Knowledge and the Tree of Life, both significant symbols for the theme of the book.

However, I would emphasise that the opinions in the book are mine and in no way do they reflect the opinions of the people who have assisted in the book.

I thank Kathryn for her unfailing support in my writings. Also thanks to our dog Darcy who sat faithfully beside my writing desk, page after page.

Kevin Treston 2013

CHAPTER ONE

Preamble

Evolution is a light which illuminates all facts, a curve that all lines must follow.

Pierre Teilhard de Chardin (1881-1955)

If only Adam and Eve had done the right thing in the beginning and obeyed God, we would all be so much better off today. Just look at the mess in the world!

Quote from a friend who was bemoaning the moral chaos in the world.

This first chapter sets out the overall plan of the book and considers seven basic issues that offer a context for an appreciation of the theme of the book.

The focus of the book is an explanation of an interpretation of the Genesis origin myth (Genesis 1-3) as the beginning of the long evolutionary journey of humankind and its implications for the Christ story and the wider global consciousness. The basic premise of the book proposes that the Genesis primeval saga may be interpreted as a story of Emergence of humankind within the evolutionary process of creation. Such an interpretation offers an alternative interpretation to the traditional understanding of the Genesis origin myth as a Fall from grace. The theme of Emergence considers how the evolutionary journey of the human species and creation impacts on the Christian story.

By 'Fall' we mean the traditional Christian interpretation in the Genesis origin myth (Genesis 2- 3) as a transition of the first humans Adam and Eve from innocent obedience to God to a condition of guilty disobedience. In the Hebrew Scriptures, the Adam and Eve myth is never referred to as the Fall. The term 'Fall' is a theological not a biblical term.

An enduring theme throughout the whole book is the scientifically demonstrated reality of evolution in an emerging universe, human species and all living things. Evolution is not a theory. It is a fact. Evolution is one of the most important discoveries of the last 150 years. Evolution with its basic notions of process, change and development affects more than biology (Phipps: 9). Evolution affects cultural change, social sciences, ecology, religion, economics, spirituality, genetics and of course science. According to the Jesuit and palaeontologist Teilhard de Chardin (1881-1955), *Evolution is a light which illuminates all facts, a curve that all lines must follow.*

The evolutionary paradigm challenges all the great religious traditions, including Christianity, both to hold fast to their essential charism and also discern how best their revelation can enhance the wellbeing of all things in creation. In the light of evolutionary science, what culturally bound beliefs, religious practices and structures need to be modified or even discarded? If Christianity is serious about its core belief in the Incarnation (John 1:14) by proclaiming that God entered the human condition in Jesus who became the Christ, then Christianity must take seriously the distilled findings of evolutionary science on the emergence of the human species.

At this point, I wish to clarify the term "Jesus who became the Christ". Much of the confusion among Christians about this term arises in liturgical prayer and in preaching where the designation 'Jesus Christ' is used as if 'Christ' were some kind of surname for the historical Jesus. New Testament writings also use the designation 'Jesus Christ' (e.g. Romans 5:17). We need to distinguish between the historical Jesus who lived, preached and died in Palestine in the first century of the Common Era (CE) and the Christ of eternity. 'Christ', meaning the 'anointed one', is a Christian descriptive name for the manifestation of the Divine in creation. 'The Christ' is more than the earthly Jesus and reflects a Christian belief about the Risen Christ pervading all of creation. The Pauline writings speak about Christ as, *He is the image of the invisible God, the first born of all creation* (Colossians 1:15).

The exploration of the theme of the book begins by setting a framework for examining the origin myth through a discussion of several 'scaffolding' issues. Each issue explains some topic which illuminates a later analysis of the Genesis origin myth. The 'scaffolding' issues for discussion include the following topics: the role of stories in religious mythology, the meaning of myth, the evolution of consciousness, hermeneutics, language and religion, science and religion, the meaning of emergence, the evolution of the universe and human species.

After examining a number of scaffolding issues relevant to the theme of the book in the first two chapters, the third chapter analyses the problems for the Christian narrative that arose when the origin myth was understood in a literal rather than a mythical mode. The traditional Christian literal understanding of the origin myth is distinctly unhelpful to the Christian narrative for at least six reasons, namely,

1. It did not take into account the legitimacy of an evolutionary understanding of the world and the human species.

2. It focused exclusively on a Judeo-Christian story that does not embrace

the universal scope of diverse divine revelations through the ages.

3. It affirmed the sacrifice/ appeasement/atonement themes in relationships with God.

4. It focused on the mission of Jesus as a restoration enterprise rather than a transformational experience.

5. It endorsed a mode of literalism rather than a mythical mode in communicating the origin story and dogmas generally.

6. It acted as an impediment to an evolutionary development of church teachings, ministry and ecclesial structures.

The later chapters consider how the theme of Emergence rather than Fall offers a useful and alternative context for the Christian story. The 'signs of the times' chapter delves into a selection of Western cultural movements in a rapidly changing world as a context for a contemporary Christian narrative. Chapter seven reflects on the Jesus story and the Christian community within a perspective of Emergence.

The final chapter suggests an evolutionary way forward for the Christian community.

To assist in appreciating the core theme of the book, the diagram below illustrates the paradigm shift in God's revelation in Jesus according to the traditional interpretation of the Genesis origin myth as Fall to an Emergence interpretation of the myth. No schema can capture the complexity or nuances of the paradigm shift. However, the diagram may orientate the reader to the general movement in consciousness emanating from the traditional interpretation of the Fall to a story of Emergence.

Genesis origin myth

Theological Themes	Traditional Interpretation	Evolutionary Interpretation
GENESIS ORIGIN STORY	Fall from grace	Emergence of consciousness
GOD	Punishment	Divine Energy of Life
HUMAN	Sinners	Graced beings
LIFE	Making reparation	Explorers of new horizons
JESUS	Rescuer	Icon of divinity/humanity

MISSION	Saviour	Abundance of life
FOCUS	Suffering	Good News
DEATH	Punishment	Transition to new life
RESURRECTION	Reward	New phase of being
EUCHARIST	Sacrifice	Celebration of community
SALVATION	Attaining heaven	Becoming whole
WORLD	Exile	Towards justice
CREATION	Backdrop to being Christian	Active earth citizenship

Let us now turn to consider the elements in the scaffolding themes.

Scaffolding themes

Before discussing an interpretation of the Genesis origin myth as a movement towards an evolution of consciousness rather than a Fall, it is helpful to construct a series of scaffolding themes which offer a context for the exploration of the Genesis myth as Emergence rather than Fall. Each of the themes in the scaffolding explores a feature of how an interpretation of the origin myth shapes the Christian story in our contemporary world.

The themes in the scaffolding are as follows:

- an understanding of myths;
- the role of stories in religious consciousness;
- evolution of consciousness;
- hermeneutics or how texts are understood in their cultural context;
- language and religion;
- science and religion;
- understanding emergence;
- evolution of the universe;
- evolution of the human species.

It is helpful to begin a consideration of the themes in the scaffolding by first raising several critical issues which need to be explained.

The first issue is to emphasise that the theme of the book is **not** an esoteric exercise in theological semantics that is remote from the lives of ordinary Christians. People soon tire of religious nitpicking when so many personal and social happenings cry out for attention. Does anyone care about biblical literalism if abandoned children cry themselves to sleep without the solace of a parent's comforting presence or 15,000 children die each day from drinking polluted water?

At first sight, the topic may seem light years away from such life happenings as family relations, household budgets, natural disasters, daily work, iPads, environmental concerns, health issues, unemployment and so on. However, a closer look at the theme of the book suggests that the topic has significant implications for life generally and certainly for Christian living. All religions, including Christianity, can and do make significant contributions to assist people in uncovering deep meaning in their life journeys. The loss of interior meaning is a major source of angst in Western cultures. A looming ecological crisis is calling humanity back to recover its psychic and spiritual rootedness in the earth. Through cyber technology, people now have an avalanche of information but do people have a world view which offers a meaningful life context for this surfeit of information? Science has uncovered the mysteries of the human genome but seems powerless to check a spike in youth suicide.

We all need viable origin myths to make sense of life's ebb and flow of each day. Questions such as the following shape the direction of our lives:

- Where have we come from?
- What is our life purpose?
- What motivates me to engage creatively in the challenges of my life journey?

Origin stories provide a meaningful framework for people in diverse cultural environments. Origin stories tell us about our life purpose and our place in the universe. The collapse of the traditional Genesis origin myth in the Western world as a source of a meaning system leaves people vulnerable to the addictions of consumerism and eco-vandalism. In their own origin stories, indigenous people were grounded in embodied participation within the integrity of creation. They invite Western peoples both to critique their consumerist addictions and compose new earth membership narratives. Unfortunately for most indigenous people, their traditional origin myths are now being shredded by the dominant consumerist myths of modern civilisation.

The second issue is related to an understanding of the mission of Christ. If the Genesis origin sacred story is interpreted as an evocative story about the emergence in the long evolutionary journey of people instead of a fall from grace, then the Christ story assumes a different perspective from a more traditional dominant one in Christology. Rather than understanding Jesus as Christ doing a divine rescue mission from an original plan for humanity that failed because of Adam and Eve's disobedience, in an evolutionary perspective, the Christ story puts more emphasis on how divinity and humanity are fused into an evolutionary journey of wholeness towards 'life in abundance' (John 10:10) for everybody and everything. The mission of Jesus as Christ is not a backward looking enterprise to rectify a purported primal fault but a forward looking endeavour to inaugurate the reign of God, a time of universal peace and justice. The Christ story has to be rescued from the literalism of interpreting the Genesis origin myth.

When we clarify the mission of Jesus, we are in a better position to affirm the role of the church in the world. In cooperation with other religious traditions and caring groups, the church is a faith community committed to enhance the wellbeing of people and creation. The church is not an end in itself. The church exists **for** the common good including the web of life in creation. According to the Lutheran pastor Dietrich Bonhoeffer, executed by the Nazis in 1945, *The church is her true self only when she exists for humanity* (166). The church's role is to act as a leaven in society for fostering wholesome values and revealing God's presence in the world. Although the essence of God's revelation in Jesus as Christ remains a unique cornerstone for Christian beliefs, the structures and teachings of the church are always in a process of evolution within an Emergence perspective. Many people are crying out for spiritual sustenance. How well does the church respond to these cries? Has the church, at least in the Western world, lost its capacity to discover new language and imagination to express God's revelation in Jesus? Or is the church offering old answers for new questions?

A third issue in interpreting the Genesis myth as Emergence rather than Fall is related to an understanding of the nature of the person (anthropology). The doctrine of original sin which evolved out of the Fall myth some four centuries after Christ taught that we begin life in a state of sin as a consequence of the Fall. This doctrine fostered a negative anthropology, that is, we start life as alienated from God. When we first gaze on the miracle of a new born baby, why are Christians required to believe that this child is born into a personal sinful state? Little wonder that so much of Christian teachings have been concerned with the individual getting out of a sinful state and saving one's soul. Why not uphold a faith perspective which insists that we begin life as a celebration of being born in original grace? While Christians uphold beliefs about original grace, the harsh reality of evil and sin in the world present challenges to comprehend the paradox of God's love in a world which is both beautiful and also morally flawed.

A fourth issue is the relationships between religion and science. Science takes things apart to discover how they work while religion brings the parts together to discover what they mean. (Sacks: 2). Scientific research on the development of the human species shows that *Homo sapiens* (wise person) evolved over thousands of years from different genetic strands. Such research negates the possibility of monogenesis (humanity descended from one couple). While few theologians would quibble with the concept of polygenesis (more than one parent group), the official church teaching is still ambivalent on questions relating to the evolution of the human species. In 1950, Pope Pius XII described evolution as a serious hypothesis worthy of in-depth investigation (*Humani Generis*). In 1996, Pope Paul II, in a conference at the Pontifical Council of Sciences, said that in view of new evidence, evolution is more than a hypothesis. However, the authors of the *Catechism of the Catholic Church* (1994) simply ignored the topic of evolution. There is no mention of evolution in the 803 pages of the *Catechism*.

To what extent is the scientific account of the evolution of humans compatible with the traditional interpretation of the Genesis origin myth as Fall? The teaching church will ignore scientifically demonstrated research at its peril. The church must articulate an intellectually responsible account of the Christian faith.

A fifth issue is concerned with exploring the implications of the origin myth as a story about the evolutionary journey of emerging levels of consciousness. As humankind moves to new levels of consciousness, so do cultural attitudes change. It would seem that we are on the threshold of a radical new level of consciousness characterised by such features as globalisation, universal cyber communications, connectedness of all things in creation, interfaith dialogue, ecological awareness, gender equity, growing disparity of wealth distribution, dispersion of democratic ideals and so on.

A sixth issue is the whole problem of dismantling the dominance of literalism in popular and dogmatic Christianity. A growing educated Western orientated population is rejecting religious proclamations that emanate from a literalist mode. A literalist mode of teaching dogma insists that beliefs such as physical bodily ascensions, an interventionist God, are facts rather than symbolic expressions of God's presence. Dogmas that contradict common sense will be discarded. The symbolic dimension of religious experience must be recovered for people to enter more fully the mystery of the numinous world.

A seventh issue is that the focus of the book relates to Western orientated countries. Some themes in the book would have little or no relevance to countries such as China or Kenya. Although there is a wide diversity of religious beliefs, religious indifference, inter-faith relations, multiculturalism and atheism in Western orientated countries, there are some basic shared values associated with democracy and cultural pluralism. A gradual awakening to the wisdoms of indigenous spiritualities and world views is also stimulating those in Western countries to critique the consequences of societies driven by the ideologies of capitalism, rationalism and consumerism.

Several questions such as the following arise out of a consideration of the interpretation of the Genesis myth as Emergence not as Fall:

- How might the life journeys of people be enriched by the wisdoms of the great religious traditions, including Christianity?
- What was (is) the mission of Christ and how does this mission shape the lives of Christians?
- Who are we as human beings? How does a holistic Christian anthropology contribute to affirming the dignity of people and fostering the common good?
- How is the reality of evil and sinfulness explained?
- How might the Christian story express and articulate its core beliefs in a symbolic rather than a literalist mode?
- How might science and religion work together in partnership for the wellbeing of humankind and creation?
- What are the implications for the diverse religious traditions, including Christianity, within the context of an evolutionary perspective on the charisms (core worldviews) of the various religions?
- How might Christianity respond to the emergence of a new consciousness that is global in its scope?

Let us consider each of these themes in the scaffolding and consider their relevance to the Genesis myth interpreted as Emergence and not as Fall.

CHAPTER TWO

Myths, stories and consciousness

This chapter examines the meaning of religious myths and the role of stories in communicating religious beliefs. The crucial role of consciousness in how religions approach and celebrate their core message is discussed. The different levels of consciousness in living religiously pose real challenges for unity in the Christian community. Other scaffolding issues such as hermeneutics, religious language, science and religion and understanding the science of emergence, all offer a useful framework to situate an analysis of the Genesis origin myth of the Fall.

Understanding myths

An exploration of the Genesis origin myth assumes an appreciation of the meaning of 'myth'. What do we mean by speaking about the Genesis origin story as a sacred myth?

If we asked people in the street, 'What do you understand by myth?', they probably would say something like this, 'It's something that's not true, a kind of fairy tale'. Recently, I heard a politician describing a government report of misappropriation of funds as 'a complete myth', meaning the report was totally false. Popular wisdom considers myths as something like children's stories such as Cinderella or Little Red Riding Hood. The meaning of myths in religious culture is very different from a popular understanding of myth. Myths are not history. Myths belong to the world of imagination and the spirit. Ancient myths were concerned with explaining the great mysteries of life. When mythological religious stories are understood as factual accounts of what happened, the theological message is lost.

By 'myth' we mean a story that is expressed in symbolic language but contains an essential truth. Western literalism finds it difficult to deal with myth. Western philosophy, following the heritage of the Greeks and Descartes, is highly rational and cognitive. The perennial question about sacred stories in Western thought is 'Is it true?' whereas the real question for appreciating a sacred myth is 'What does it mean?' We need to express religious truths primarily in mythical language because our literalism can never capture the depth of the divine mystery. In his teachings Jesus spoke in metaphors and symbols to communicate to us the wonder of God's revelation. The parables are symbolic stories, illustrating the reign of God.

The Genesis origin myth describes in symbolic language God's revelation in creation and the moral ambivalence of human existence. The opening chapters of Genesis intend to present a symbolic account of a loving God creating the world while seeking to explain the causes of sin and misery that were caused by human failure and not according to God's will.

A major problem arose in the Christian tradition when the symbolism of the myth was subverted by literalism and the doctrinal framework which evolved out of this literalism. Western Christianity or perhaps all Christianity urgently needs to recover an appreciation of the world of *mythos* if it is going to communicate the gospel effectively. The prospects for Christianity are bleak if it communicates God's revelation out of a literalist mode within a scientific cultural environment.

Although it would appear that the Western world has a diminished sense of *mythos*, the role of *logos* or rational thinking should not be ignored. Healthy religious beliefs and practices need both *mythos* and *logos*. *Logos* is pragmatic and logical, enabling people to make decisions and formulate beliefs. *Logos* initiates practical programs for justice, pastoral planning, articulate theology, canon law and ecological sustainability. During the late Middle Ages there was a growing movement in theology for a greater emphasis on empiricism or grounding theology in a pragmatic mode. This movement was augmented with the rise of scientific method after the 16th century.

Attaining a balance between *mythos* and *logos* in religious thinking and living without confusing the two realms of religious experience is an imperative for religious credibility in a modern world. If people are asked to believe certain religious statements literally such as, 'he descended into hell' (Apostles Creed) instead of appreciating this creedal statement as a symbolic expression of Christ's redemptive presence in and beyond world, then religious beliefs face a credibility dilemma. Unless people appreciate the levels of *mythos* and *logos* in religious language, they can too readily dismiss Christian beliefs as a whole series of fables.

To illustrate the intersection of *mythos* and *logos*, consider the nativity story as told in the gospels of Luke and Matthew. At the *logos* level, Bethlehem is named as the birth place of Jesus and most scripture scholars uphold this tradition. However, in recent times, some scripture writers have proposed that Jesus was born in his home town of Nazareth, rather than in Bethlehem. Such writers would contend that the idea of everyone in the vast Roman Empire being required to travel to their place of birth for census purposes is preposterous and there is no record of such a census decree. Furthermore, the notion of the heavily pregnant Mary travelling on a donkey an arduous 150 kilometres from Nazareth to Bethlehem is unthinkable, and so on.

However, at the level of *mythos,* the nativity story is a wondrous story of God's affinity with the little ones of the world, vulnerability, animals as symbols of creation, God's presence in the angels, the universalism of Jesus the Christ with the visit of the wise men, links with the city of David and so on. The telling of the Christian story needs *mythos* and *logos* and the wisdom to know the difference between them.

Those who participate in Christmas Eve Mass with its nativity scene are not really interested in *logos* questions about the historical veracity of the nativity story. Rather, they become immersed in the evocative power of *mythos* which celebrates God with us. Who is not touched by the children's joy in the acting out the roles of Mary, Joseph, shepherds and angels in the Christmas Eve nativity pageant? Surely singing Christmas carols is hardly the time to weigh up erudite arguments for and against the respective claims of Bethlehem or Nazareth as the birth place of Jesus!

The role of stories

Since the beginning of human consciousness, people have wondered about the mysteries of life with such questions as:

- Where did we come from?
- Why do we exist?
- Why is there suffering?
- What happens to us after death?
- Is the universe directed by a divine being?
- How do we appease and gain favours from divine powers?
- What is the relationship of humans to the world?
- What does it mean to live given the fact that one day I will die?

Throughout thousands of years, tribes have told communal stories to make sense of their world as responses to these questions. All cultures have origin stories. One such origin story is the myth of Genesis, Chapters 1- 3.

Stories are an integral feature of the human psyche. We all have innate desires to tell stories of our experiences and make sense of the mysteries of life. Everyone has personal narratives which tell us who we are and where we have come from. Stories link our past and present. There is a kind of magical attraction in the conversation statement, 'Once upon a time...' or 'You will never believe what happened to me...' Tribal groups have handed down stories about their origins and tribal identity for thousands of years. Humans have at their disposal a treasure of accumulated wisdom gathered over many years to pass on to future generations. Stories offer an inner connectedness within humanity that transcends ethnic, tribal and religious boundaries of time and place.

Stories connect us to a larger world and give meaning to our existence. On my first visit to our family farm in October 1972 in County Mayo, Ireland, I recall the feeling of inner connectedness when the hired car I was driving turned into the road leading to our ancestral farm. My grandfather had left this farm in July 1879 to make the long voyage to Townsville, Australia. When I visited the family cemetery at Cloontreston, I read the inscriptions telling me about my foremothers and forefathers in centuries past. The tombstones were a silent reminder to me of a personal connectedness with family generations long ago. Communal stories are like links to a chain of family heritages. Likewise religious stories provide a framework of meaning in the face of the mysteries of life and our relationship with the divine powers.

There are good and bad stories. An example of a bad story was the Nazi narrative about the supremacy of a master race. During World War II, this shocking story dispatched millions of people to the obscenity of the Holocaust. In contrast to a bad story, a good story provides a group with a kind of 'cantus firmus' or basic melody, which shapes the values and ethical norms of tribal life. A 'cantus firmus' has no harmony or counterpoint in its musical score. A 'cantus firmus' for a culture is the reference point for beliefs, rituals and worship in the religious system of the group. Good cultural stories tell of themes which are essential for people of that culture to know about their origins and communal values. Good cultural stories are attuned to the levels of consciousness within particular social environments.

With the current explosion of knowledge through cyber technology, we are now in a position of having access to global knowledge and hence the capacity to explore levels of consciousness which bypass national and ethnic boundaries. For example, people who live in cultures which are strongly shaped by patriarchy now have access to information about gender equity. The global scope of cyber technology offers people a real prospect of universality in cultural stories.

A growing feature of the modern world is interreligious dialogue because people can easily gain information about different religious traditions. Through migration, particular religious groups are no longer confined to specific geographical areas. World religions narrate sacred stories that transcend cultural, ethnic and national boundaries. The Christian narrative is not isolated from other narratives relating to cultural stories, religious traditions and the story of the universe.

Religions no longer control their narratives as undisputed truth. Through the internet, other narratives are accessed and evaluated against specific religious narratives. People in Western orientated cultures now can operate in a 'pick-and-choose' environment and make faith decisions according to their own evaluation of a belief system. The idea of accepting the whole corpus of Christian doctrines without any reservation or question is not a concept that sits easily with the individual choice mentality and education of Western orientated Christians. If the Catholic tradition of rationality is honoured, then this tradition of rationality is contradicted by those church leaders who insist on absolute obedience without coherent explanations of doctrinal proclamations. The rise of democracy during the last two hundred years has further eroded the legitimacy of an imperial model of church to suppress dissenting voices.

The speed of change in world events and consciousness is happening so rapidly that religions are now challenged to draw new maps that chart their narratives through an avalanche of easily accessible information. I believe that future social historians will agree that the late 20th century was a defining era in the evolution of consciousness. Virtually every item of information can now be obtained by the click of a mouse. For most of its history, the church controlled the dissemination of information about its history and teachings. That era of censorship of religious thinking has now been bypassed by the internet. Church teachings have to stand scrutiny in the glare of public media. Static and pre-scientific age images of God will be dismissed by new generations of scientifically formed Christians unless people are helped to appreciate the power and relevance of myth in how beliefs are expressed in their Christian faith.

When people say, 'I believe in God', who is the God or what is the image of divinity are they invoking? Does an interventionist divine power that pops in and out of human events have credence for people today? Is 'God' the divine power that is invoked to win a football match or organise a sunny day for the parish carnival? When the gospels record Jesus walking across the waters during a raging storm in the Sea of Galilee, what does that miracle story mean? Did Jesus have some kind of floats tied to his feet enabling him to walk across waves? When the Catholic Church proclaims, 'Mary was assumed body and soul into heaven at the Assumption', what does that dogmatic statement mean? At the level of *mythos*, there would appear to be no problem for Catholics or Orthodox Christians with beliefs about the holiness of Mary and her transformed human existence. On the other hand, to proclaim as a dogma the bodily assumption of Mary to heaven in any literalist mode evokes the obvious question, 'If Mary was bodily assumed into heaven, where does the body of Mary now reside?' When dogmas are understood literally, they lose their essential religious meaning.

Faced with a world shaped by science and rapid shifts in cultural consciousness, religions have to revise their core charisms and articulate their message in symbols and language that are understood within a cultural environment. A younger generation is now so immersed in science that any religion that does not deal with the intersection point between science and the world of *mythos* will be regarded as belonging to a bygone pre-scientific era. The questions posed by apologists such as Stephen Hawking or Richard Dawkins for an exclusive scientific world view cannot be casually dismissed by religious shibboleths.

Consciousness and religious understanding

By 'consciousness' I mean how the mind interprets its experiences. The idea that human consciousness has evolved is well attested in history. The interior world of the human person is evolving just as the external world is evolving. A reading of history illustrates how cultural groups have very different worldviews. Cultural change happens when prophetic people envisage an alternative way of looking at cultural norms. Just consider the worldviews of social groups throughout the ages about such themes as the human body, the world of spirits, the concept of democracy, slavery, status of women, divine right of kings, arranged marriages, tribalism and so on.

I recall reading about a pilot's observations as he was flying over a vast Canadian forest with two passengers, one a member of the Blackfoot tribe and the other a logging magnate. The logging magnate was estimating the millions of dollars waiting below in forest harvesting. The indigenous person sat quietly reflecting on the sacred sites in the forests below. It seems that the evolution of consciousness moves in leaps and bounds and does not necessarily occur in an ordered sequence. In our era, it would seem that a significant leap in consciousness is happening and happening very quickly. Humankind seems to crossing a threshold into a new consciousness involving an understanding of the oneness of the planetary system.

In recent scientific research, there has emerged a range of speculations about the possibility of an expanded appreciation of a universal or common consciousness. New science, in the form of quantum physics, proposes that everything in the universe is interrelated and the driving force of change is not matter but consciousness. The notion of a universal consciousness, also called 'transpersonal consciousness', acts as a connecting link with everything in the universe.

Indigenous mythology has always assumed the connectedness of everything in the world that breathes or does not breathe. The 12th century mystic, Hildegard of Bingen, expressed this interconnectedness of all things by writing, 'Everything that is in the heavens, in the earth, and under the earth is penetrated with connectedness, penetrated with relatedness'. From his work with patients, the Swiss psychologist Carl Jung (1875-1961) described how there seemed to be a deep layer of a common consciousness that transcended personal consciousness. He called this universal consciousness 'collective unconsciousness'. Jung believed that everyone is connected to an interior universal realm of our psyche, the 'collective unconscious'.

A prominent physicist David Bohm (early 20th century) stated, 'We have to regard the universe as an undivided and unbroken whole'. Because of the interconnectedness of all things, there is only one common consciousness and our own consciousness is part of this common consciousness. If there is a common consciousness, then every individual action or thought we have affects every other person in the world (Smith 2008:44). The core message of Jesus, the reign of God, is an expression of this universal consciousness, a dream of equality and justice for all humanity, not only for the followers of Jesus.

Currently there is a dramatic shift in consciousness in Western influenced countries. The new levels of consciousness have significant implications on how religions communicate their message. The globalisation movement encourages the great religious traditions to transcend denominationalism and their unique claims to absolute truth. The history of religions tells how often specific religious traditions make claims that they, and they alone, possess absolute truth. Such exclusive claims to truth have caused untold misery to those who suffer from the consequences of religious intolerance.

Western consciousness is far removed in time and character from biblical assumptions about religious truth. Pre-scientific views are still held by fundamentalist Christians in Western countries. However, it must be emphasised that scientific truth does not hold a monopoly on truth nor is truth absolute, neither in science or in religion. Albert Einstein once wrote that 'all truth is relative'. Science probes the mysteries of the universe. Religion probes the mysteries of the divine presence in creation. For a religious person, the ultimate and final truth is in God or a Presence beyond human comprehension. Scientific and religious truths should be partners in the great quest for wisdom. Science and religion are complementary modes of thought. Each has its own assumptions about reality. An awareness of levels of consciousness is a vital feature of appreciating the essential charisms of religious stories. The Genesis origin story epitomises the challenge of reconciling the deep religious truths imbedded in the origin myth with the insights of modern science about the evolution of the universe and the human species.

The universe, like us, is in a constant state of evolution. In an evolutionary perspective, we are always in the process of *becoming*. Theories, ideas and religious doctrines are always in a process of change, at least in the ways that they are expressed at any one point of historical time. In the Middle Ages, the most eminent theologian in the Christian church, Thomas Aquinas (1225c-1274), could write that one of the delights of heaven for the blessed was observing how God's justice is meted out to those burning in hell (Friedrich Nietzsche [1844-1900] *Genealogy of Morals First Essay* 15). While such theology might be acceptable in his time, this very notion is revolting for Christians in the 21st century.

- Is it possible to reconcile evolutionary theories about humankind with the religious truths of the sacred myth of Genesis?

Levels of consciousness

People are aware of the different levels of consciousness such as being awake, dreaming, altered states of consciousness induced by meditation or drugs or a deep consciousness. People have visions and gain insight into personal issues through dreams. Dreams are the symbolic language of our unconscious. The world of the transcendent and numinous is as real as the scientific world. Elizabeth Nowotny-Keane in her insightful book *Amazing Encounters*, recounts stories of people who have received direct visits and communications from deceased loved ones. Spiritual energy is integral to the very essence of the nature of being human.

In more recent times, theorists such as Wilber, Piaget, Levinson, Baldwin, Maslow, Gilligan, Fowler and Kohlberg have developed theories about a movement upwards of stages of consciousness. A general upwards movement is characterised by a progression from a Parent-Child level to a Tribal level to a level of living with Paradox and finally to an Integral level of consciousness. The scope of integral consciousness is global in scope and offers new paths towards a higher level of the interior life (Smith 6-7). The Integral level of consciousness brings together the experience of the divine, creation and humanity into a holistic vision of life. The dynamic interrelatedness of the divine, human and creation will be developed later in the book, especially in relationship to the 'cosmotheandric' vision of reality as described by the interreligious theologian Ramon Panikkar (1918-2010).

The anthropologist Jean Gebser proposed five stages of consciousness: archaic, magic, mythic, rational and integral. States of consciousness come and go but stages of consciousness are permanent (Wilber: 5). Once a person reaches a certain stage of consciousness, this stage stays with the person. A personal crisis, such as a death in family, serious illness, breakdown of significant relationship may trigger a person to incorporate a previous stage and move to a higher level of consciousness. A person may be motivated to move from a 'me' centred level of thinking to a 'group' or 'tribal' level of thinking and then finally to a 'world' perspective. On the other hand, a person may become fixated at the 'me' level and remain narcissistic throughout his or her life. Selfish people believe the world revolves around them.

Religious leaders aspire to lead followers to a 'world' or 'divine' view of the oneness of creation in God. The gospels speak about the call of Jesus for 'conversion' or *metanoia* (Greek: *meta* 'beyond' and *noia* 'mind', that is, 'to go beyond the mind'). To 'go beyond the mind' is a movement to a new level of consciousness beyond our own egos into the universal consciousness of God and the Oneness of all things in creation. For a Christian, the 'going beyond the mind' towards a universal consciousness in God might be called 'Christ consciousness'. The preaching of Jesus about the reign of God was a movement towards a new consciousness where the divine and human would be energised by the power of love into Christ consciousness. Paul urges people not to be, *conformed to this world, but be transformed by the renewing of your minds, so that you may discern what is the will of God* (Romans 12:2) (MacGregor:132).

The concept of stages of consciousness is not a new idea. Over 2000 years ago, the Chinese philosopher Confucius designated six stages in the life journey, culminating in the sixth stage as 'Following the Heart'. St Teresa of Avila (1515-1582) wrote about the spiritual journey through living in the 'interior castles'. A traditional understanding of the path of Christian spirituality, attributed to Maximus the Confessor (580-665), envisaged three steps: the purgative way (turning away from sin and confronting addictions), the illuminative way (focusing on Christ and discernment) and the unitive way (finding union with God).

The history of religions amply demonstrates the significance of levels of consciousness in living religiously. Some religious people express their religious faith at such a low level of consciousness that they deny the very heart of their religious tradition. Sadly the history of religions is replete with many instances of religious people who have murdered, raped and pillaged in the name of some god - Jesus, Allah or Krishna. There is something quite obscene in reading news reports about fundamentalist Christians attacking gay people or Islamic suicide bombers screaming, 'Allahu Akbar' ('God is great') while they blow into oblivion innocent people who are attending the funeral of their loved ones.

Hermeneutics and sacred interpretation

All the great religions espouse sacred stories which invite their people to move from external practices to deeper levels of consciousness where the numinous or divine may be encountered. After thousands of years, the oral transmission of religious stories began to be recorded in a written mode. How the written texts were handed down to future generations and how the stories are received pose problems for interpretation. For example, how do we now understand texts in the Hebrew Scripture which endorses slavery, child sacrifice, divinely commanded massacres of defeated foes and subordination of women? How do readers of later texts distil the religious messages in the texts without denying the authenticity of the core revelation of the Bible?

The principle of hermeneutics examines biblical texts to better appreciate their cultural context, why the texts were composed and how the editing of the texts happened. How the so-called Fall story was interpreted left an enduring character on both the nature of human beings (anthropology) and how Christ's mission was explained. An ignorance of hermeneutics leaves readers exposed to the bane of literalism in reading a biblical text such as the story of the 'Fall'.

If those interpreting religious stories communicate the message of the stories in a literalist mode, the deep wisdoms of the stories are either lost or subverted. As the history of religions attest, it is all too common for those communicating the religious story to walk around the circumference of the words of the story and not descend to its religious heart as the axis point of the story. St Augustine (354-430) once wrote, 'The important task of the Christian life is to restore the eye of the heart by which God can be seen'. Walking around the circumference of the Christian story might involve giving priority to upholding ecclesial structures, the exercise of authority, canon law and liturgical prescriptions without discerning how each feature of church life enhances or does not enhance the proclamation of the gospel. The handling of clergy abuse situations by church authorities tragically illustrated how institutional priorities focused on upholding a sanctified image of church while ignoring the cries of the victims of abuse (c.f. Robinson).

In his public ministry, Jesus faced this very problem when he met fierce resistance from some of the religious leaders of his time. Those leaders operated from basic levels of consciousness which emphasised the letter of the Mosaic law rather than the inner religious essence of Judaism. Jesus refused to accept the purity codes which separated religious practices from the everyday lives of people and how these purity codes magnified the distinction between the holy and unholy. When Jesus healed the man with the withered hand, the Pharisees accused him of breaking the Sabbath (Mark 3:1-6). Jesus appealed to a higher level of consciousness, *Is it lawful to do good or harm on the Sabbath, to save life or to kill?* (verse 4). By this act of healing, Jesus proclaimed a living God, a God who is passionate about life. Just before his death, a furious Jesus entered the temple and drove out the buyers and sellers, crying out, *My house shall be called a house of prayer, but you are making it a den of thieves* (Matthew 21:13).

Fixated basic levels of consciousness can inhibit deep encounters with the divine. If we utilise the insights of the psychologist Carl Jung, the ever present danger for religious people is to identify the practice of religious faith with the *persona* or external form of a religious tradition rather than with the Self or *Imago Dei* or God centre of our being.

Western culture has made enormous positive contributions to the value and legal rights of the individual person. A negative aspect of this emphasis on the individual as 'you are special' is over-identification with the self or ego to the neglect of the communal self who participates in the common good. The ego is inflated by commercial interests in promoting a culture of self image and addictions to augmenting possessions. 'Shop till you drop', 'You are what you wear', 'You can have it all', become new mantras for living in a consumer environment. The wisdom of Arsene Hoosaye in his saying, 'Tell me whom or what you love and I will tell you who you are' has been replaced by 'tell me where you live and what you wear and I'll tell you who you are'.

The inner core or charism of the message of Jesus is the reign of God. The metaphor of the reign of God envisaged a world of harmony and reconciliation, a time of peace and inclusion of all people. Jesus appealed to a higher level of consciousness than was generally espoused by the dominant religious teachings of his day. His bitter opponents sought to protect the law as a system. As a devout Jew, Jesus did not reject the law but sought to transcend the law as a pathway to encounter a gracious God. The Torah, Bible or Koran or indeed any religious text or system is never an end in itself but a framework to facilitate people experiencing God's presence and love. Every Christian community needs parameters of belonging, laws and an exercise of authority. However, the ongoing temptation for religions is to so enshrine external elements of their tradition that they lose their mystical centre. The three temptations to Jesus as recorded in Matthew (4:1-10), Mark (1:12) and Luke (4:1-12) describe the temptations to choose a manifestation of power for an external good rather than power for promoting God's will.

The Bible has texts which exemplify all stages of consciousness although the general movement is from a lower to a higher level of consciousness. We will always struggle with biblical texts which are contradictory and inconsistent. Knowledge of hermeneutics is critical for making sense of contradictory texts. As it has often been said, 'You can prove anything from the Bible'. Biblical texts evolved over 1000 years and the evolution of human consciousness is self-evident from early eras of King David's time until the late first century CE. For example, compare the command of Yahweh to Joshua where Joshua, *utterly destroyed all that breathed as the Lord God of Israel commanded* (Joshua 10:40) with the Sermon on the Mount (Matthew 5:3-12). Consider the demand of God to Abraham, '*Take your son, your only son Isaac, whom you love, and go to the land of Moriah and offer him as a burnt offering on one of the mountains that I will show you* (Genesis 22:2). A transformation in consciousness at a much later era than the scribes of the Abraham story is evident when we reflect on the words of Jesus, *As the Father has loved me, so I have loved you; abide in my love* (John 15:9).

Higher levels of consciousness enable people to deal more easily with paradox, contradictions, imagination and mystery. Higher levels of consciousness minimise the need to reduce the ambivalence of living religiously into fixed boundaries of religious practice. Prophets in religious traditions often pay a heavy price for calling people in their faith tradition to think differently. If the seekers and explorers in religious traditions are banished, the integrity of that tradition is likewise diminished.

Anthony de Mello SJ's warning is a timely reminder about the urgency for discerned listening in the current climate of official church exclusions of prophetic voices, 'Those who drive out dissenters have peace but no future'. People operating from a lower level of consciousness may find it difficult to accept the good will and integrity of those who lead a faith life from a higher level of consciousness. Those who live a faith life from a higher level of consciousness can be criticised as people of 'dissent' by people of a lower level of consciousness. Such people become angry at perceived enemies of the church such as 'radical theologians, feminists and "cafeteria" Christians'.

According to these people, those who disagree with church teachings should learn humility and obey the church's teachings in all things. Likewise, people who are promoting reform in the church need to respect those of more conservative religious positions.

For people who seek to live a Christ centred life, theological categories such as 'Conservative', 'Radical', 'Modernist', 'Feminist', 'Progressive' have little meaning. A faithful church community promotes the inclusion of members who are at all levels of religious consciousness. When staying with my aged mother while working in a diocese on the topic of contemporary spirituality, I fondly recall the sight of my mother sitting in her favourite chair saying the rosary in the early hours of the morning. Who was 'conservative' or was 'progressive' – my mother or myself ? An inclusive Christian community encourages people to experience their faith lives across a whole spectrum of beliefs.

An inclusive Christian community supports its members to live their faith without rancour or pass judgment on people who respond to God in diverse ways. Christians experience their faith in a plethora of ways such as prayer, meditation, Scripture readings, liturgy, picketing as a protest against coal seam gas exploration, teaching, devotions, charitable works, caring for the homeless, soup kitchens, prisoner visitations, participation in justice projects, honesty in work, family living and so on. No one group can insist that they - and they alone - have a monopoly of the Holy Spirit! Religious exclusionism rejects the prospect of religious diversity. According to Jesus, *The wind blows where it chooses, and you hear the sound of it, but you do not know where it comes from or where it goes. So it is with everyone who is born of the Spirit* (John 3:8).

Evolution of consciousness

The evolution of consciousness has enormous implications for the wellbeing of the planet. Transpersonal consciousness makes us aware that humans are an integral part of every living thing. With the passing of time, the dynamics of the planet are increasingly affected by the influence of human consciousness (Swimme & Tucker: 66). Humans are probably now the most single influential factor in what happens to planetary health. Anthropologists, such as Stanislav Grof, describe the evolution of human consciousness in two modes, the *hylotropic* and the *holotropic* levels of consciousness. *Hylotropic* consciousness relates to every day existence and world events. *Holotropic* consciousness is consciousness at deeper levels of mysticism and wholeness. The overemphasis and social rewards in Western countries are more associated with *hylotropic* consciousness such as business, entertainment, work practices, leisure and so on. The de-emphasising of *holotropic* consciousness makes it more difficult in the West to effectively address issues relating to the root causes of the ecological crisis and loss of meaning in people's lives.

Hylotropic consciousness approaches planetary health with legislation and actions for earth care. *Holotropic* consciousness alerts people to the inner oneness and interconnectedness of everything in creation. Both levels are needed to respond effectively to the ecological crisis. We need specific actions for earth sustainability at a personal and communal level. We also need an ecological spiritual conversion energised by a vibrant eco-spirituality.

Another approach to describe the evolution of consciousness proposes three stages of consciousness. Simple stage, represented by Eden, was where humans lived in the present moment without a sense of time or space and without any understanding of themselves as separate from other beings. The first two chapters of Genesis would reflect this static Simple level of consciousness. The next stage in consciousness was Self consciousness, happening about 120,000 years ago (or later) when humans became aware of being self-reflective individuals. It would appear that language and religion could and did evolve in this second stage. The act of Adam and Eve in taking the fruit of the Tree of Knowledge reflects a symbolic movement to the stage of self-consciousness. The third stage seems to be evolving at this time and may be designated as 'Universal or Cosmic' consciousness. Cosmic consciousness involves an inner communion with the web of life on the planet and is global in its scope. In the gradual emergence of cosmic consciousness, we are slowly developing a greater awareness that humans are **within** the process of evolution. *Homo sapiens* evolved from hominids who, in turn, evolved from primal forms of life which evolved millions of years ago from stardust. If the human person is integral to the process of evolution, then we can make choices for enhancing planetary health in the future. Not only can we make choices, we are morally bound to make choices for planetary health.

Our present generation is slowly relearning that the earth is finite. We cannot keep using oceans as dumping grounds for our refuse without grave ecological consequences. Each year, 6,000 tonnes of waste are tipped into our oceans. The International Coastal Cleanup report (2008) suggested that plastic litter had increased by 126% since the first ICC survey in 1994. Humanity currently produces 83,000 different chemicals, one third of which are known or suspected to cause serious diseases such as cancer. The global output of chemicals is thirty million tonnes a year.

Certain assumptions that we have held for thousands of years about us and the earth are no longer appropriate. The assumption that the earth has been created for our benefit and our benefit alone is false. St Thomas Aquinas (1225c-1274) taught that the world was good but not good of itself. The earth was good in so far as it served the needs of humankind. In the enduring popular *Spiritual Exercises of St Ignatius* (16th century), we read, *Man has been created to praise, reverence and serve Our Lord God, thereby saving his soul. Everything else on Earth has been created for man's sake, to enable him to achieve the purpose for which he was created* (quoted from Smith 2001:66). Humans exist within the web of life in the universe and are utterly dependent on the dynamics of planetary life for their very existence. Every breath of oxygen is a gift from a creator God to humanity and all living things.

The earth is primary as a source of life. Humans are very late arrivals in the evolutionary story. Although humans are now integral to the ebb and flow of life in the universe, the planet was not created as humankind's exclusive domain. However, humans have a special role in fostering ecological sustainability. Through the evolution of self-reflection, humans are empowered to know and relate to the Divine Source of all things in creation.

Creation is about 13.7 billion years old. Primal humans are perhaps two million years old. According to Thomas Berry, the traditional story of the universe which has sustained humanity for a long period of time, is no longer an effective story. The old pre-scientific story of humans within the cosmos has been discredited by science. The old story is being replaced by a story shaped by modern cosmology and evolution. According to Berry, *We are in trouble just now because we do not have a good story. We are in between stories. The old story, the account of how the world came to be and how we fit into it, is no longer effective* (123). Have humans now reached a level of consciousness which enables them to compose a new story of us and the earth? Perhaps future planetary health will depend on humans moving to a higher level of consciousness that motivates them to live differently as caring citizens of the earth community.

Humankind witnessed a progression of consciousness from Stone Age ancestors through such 'marker' times as the Axial period (Greek 4th century BCE, Buddhism, Hinduism, Taoism), the Renaissance (15th-16th century), the Enlightenment (18th century) and the new era of consciousness beginning in the 1960s. However, another perspective on the evolution of consciousness would propose Western consciousness has been overly shaped by rationalism and individualism without a holistic vision of life in the universe (O'Murchu 38-40). In a culture shaped by rationalism and individualism, truth becomes what an individual thinks is true. Beliefs are examined critically before these beliefs are accepted. Meta-narratives about the purpose of life have lost their credibility in an age of rationalism and individualism.

Cultural stories and sacred myths are told within the lens of levels of consciousness and interpreted accordingly. If the interpretation of the cultural story no longer resonates with the levels of communal consciousness, then the story has diminished relevance for the people of that era. This very issue is a critical ingredient in the nature of the crisis in Western Christianity.

Christian teachings must be congruent with demonstrated science and cosmology. There is one truth in God, not two opposites and contradictory truths, science and religion. For example, church teaching previously stated that death entered the world through the sin of Adam and Eve. The *Catechism of the Catholic Church* states, *because of man, creation is now subject "to its bondage and decay"* (n 400). Our own experience knows that that statement does not make any sense. The cycle of birth, growth and death is a constant facet of everything in creation. Death is not a consequence of human actions from a purported act of disobedience to God in distant times. Dinosaurs became extinct sixty-five million years ago, millions of years before humans emerged.

Once again, it must be emphasised that if church teachings contradict common sense or communal lived experience, such teachings are dismissed. As a child, I recall the sadness of my mother who was forbidden by the local church to attend the funeral service of her Protestant friend. How the teachings of Jesus on inclusion became debased into such a perverted vision of the gospel is a wake-up call for all Christians to avoid such prohibitions in the future.

Language and religion

A further scaffolding theme for an exploration of the Genesis origin myth as an Emergence not Fall is the issue of language and religion. All language, especially religious language, is finite and symbolic. Religious traditions speak about God or Divine Energy that is described in human attributes. We will never really understand the mystery and transcendence of Allah, Brahma or God. No doctrine or language form can ever encapsulate the whole truth but simply point to the divine mystery that is beyond our comprehension. We can only express things about the divine presence as a metaphor. In the text *The Cloud of Unknowing* (14th century), the anonymous writer proposes that the only way of 'knowing' the divine is to let go all our preconceived notions of God and surrender to the 'unknowing' of the divine mystery (Johnston:137-138).

In the life of Thomas Aquinas, there is a moving story about the paucity of language in writing about God. Towards the end of his life, it is told that Thomas experienced some kind of vision. One day he stopped writing and put his head on the desk. His concerned scribe asked Thomas what was the matter. Thomas pointed to his voluminous writings of the *Summa* and said, 'All that writing is nothing more than straw'.

Because doctrines are expressed in a language and form of a particular era, they are always in need of re-formulation in the light of contemporary culture. The language of the Nicene Creed recited in the Mass is a good example of the dilemma faced by liturgists. The Nicene Creed was formulated as a rebuttal to prevailing heresies in the fourth century. Does the worshipping community continue to say a formula that has its philosophical origins in the fourth century or does it compose a creedal statement that is intelligible for contemporary Christians?

Recently, a well educated Catholic said to me, 'What is the point of reciting phrases such as the following in the Nicene Creed, "only begotten Son of the Father", "consubstantial with the Father", or in the Apostles Creed, "he descended into hell'? Those statements don't make any sense to me, what do they mean?' My explanations about the historical origins of fourth century Greek philosophical language of the Nicene Creed left him decidedly unimpressed. Fourth century Greek language forms are very different from modern English.

There is another related issue with creedal statements such as the Nicene Creed. The Nicene Creed is a very incomplete testament of Christian beliefs. It makes no mention of the centrality of the mission of Jesus in his preaching about the reign of God. The words of the Creed move immediately from his birth to his death, missing out the central theme of the teachings of Jesus!

St Paul was keenly aware of the difficulty of naming religious experience when he wrote, *For now, we see in a mirror dimly* (1 Corinthians 13:12). Hindu teachers speak of a God Manifest which can be described and spoken about using human symbols and language and a God Unmanifest whose identity cannot be known but only acknowledged. St Augustine of Hippo (354- 430) wrote, 'If you understand him, he is not God'. St Augustine's evocative words capture some of the profound mystery of God's indwelling when he wrote, *interior intimo meo* ('more inward to me than my inmost parts'). We recall how St Francis of Assisi (1182- 1226) wandered about crying out, 'Who are you, God, and who am I?' St John of the Cross (d 1591) once wrote, 'God refuses to be known. God can only be loved'. Rather than aspire to reduce the mystery of God to closed doctrinal formulas, we might be better served in our spiritual life by allowing the mystery of God to enfold us.

Although we have to use language in communicating religious beliefs and worship, we learn to use religious language with all its limits and reservations.

Language in worship should reflect cultural understandings of the language. Why did the authors of the revised liturgy of 2011 insist in using the gender exclusive word 'men' in the Nicene Creed instead of a gender inclusive word such as 'us'? The word 'men' in contemporary culture refers exclusively to male gender. Why should a literal translation of the Latin word take precedence over inclusive language in worship?

Sometimes on a clear night I gaze with awe and wonder at the night sky with its vast canopy of stars in the Milky Way. Such a vision moves me to ponder on the Divine Spirit of creation moving through and within the universe with its billions of galaxies and stars. I marvel at the genius of nature where the Australian lyrebird can not only copy avian songs of twenty-five species of bird songs but can do the mimicking so accurately that the copied bird species cannot tell the difference between their songs and the lyrebird copying. I am in awe of how the Brazil nut tree is perpetuated by a rodent chewing through the tough outer nut shell and planting the seed across the rain forest floor.

We recognise the paucity of any language which assumes to speak with finality about a Creator God. The history of religion illustrates how frequently the word 'God' or 'Divine Energy' or 'Allah' is locked into specific belief systems that can so readily limit spiritual encounters. If we are absolutely certain that we know who God is, we are probably describing an idol of deity which is created in our own image and likeness. God made humanity in God's image and likeness. Humanity reversed the favour and so often makes 'god' in human image and likeness.

The word 'original sin' for designating the mystery of evil in the world is an example of a poor choice of language. The word 'sin' seems to imply culpability. A new born child is certainly not morally culpable or in a state of sin but born into original grace, created in the image and likeness of God. The child is born with a nature that is inclined to both goodness and selfishness. A child is also born into a morally ambivalent world with all its beauty and chaos, its loves and hates, its propensity for good and for evil. The global manifestations of evil in the twentieth century left deep scars on the Western psyche (Johnson: 50-51). Auschwitz has become a symbol of the face of sin and evil. The church needs to formulate a more appropriate language than 'original sin' to describe the capacity of each person to sin and the mystery of evil in the world. No one doubts the reality of sin and evil. What language best describes the reality of personal and structural sin?

Science and religion

During the last few decades, research into such areas of science such as genetics, cosmology, anthropology and biology have advanced so rapidly that it is almost impossible to be even generally conversant with major developments. Science governs every facet of our lives and has brought enormous benefits to humankind through such advances in transport, communications, food production, health and earth care. Science has also casts a long shadow across the globe with such developments as nuclear weapons, easy access to cyber bullying, manipulation of financial markets and ecological vandalism.

An enduring issue between science and religion is the relationship between God or a divine presence and the physical universe. Does God act within the evolutionary process of the unfolding universe or does God just remain aloof and let the dynamics of evolution take its course? If God does not interact with the evolving universe, where does that leave Christian beliefs about God as creator Spirit? If God does intervene in the process of evolution, where does that leave the integrity of science to uncover the mysteries of the universe? (Worthington in Regan and Worthington 153-156). There are no easy answers to the dilemma of where science and religious faith interact in evolution. Both science and religion need to respect each other's assumptions about reality and explore how each can better the quality of life in all of creation.

Religion and science both seek truth. To be faithful to the quest for truth, both science and religion have to return again and again to seek their version of truth anew as new insights, scientific discoveries and new knowledge emerge. According to Chief Rabbi and philosopher Jonathan Sacks, *Science is the search for explanations. Religion is the search for meaning* (37). There is no such thing as 'settled science'. Newtonian physics was largely overturned in the 20th century by quantum physics. New scientific discoveries regularly make previous research obsolete.

A general public view is that the realms of religion and science are mutually exclusive. However, for most of human history, religion and science operated out of an underlying philosophical and religious unity. Tragically for both science and religion, their ways significantly parted especially after the 17th century. Unlike earlier times, in the last few centuries it is now science, not religion, which assumes to posses the greater authority to truth and it is religion that has to justify itself, at least in Western cultures. Only in modern times has there been some tenuous reconciliation between science and religion. For almost three hundred years science lost its soul and religion lost its intellectual character. The stories of Copernicus, Galileo and Darwin, to name but a few, are well known in illustrating the breakdown in relations between science and religion.

However, one needs to offer a word of caution about over generalisations concerning the divorce between religion and science. The dichotomy between science and religion was never definitive. In the first half of the nineteenth century, many of the scientists were clergy. When we consider, for example, the investigative work in genetics by an Augustinian priest Mendel (1822-1884), the research of the Belgian priest Lemaitre (1884-1966) who was the first scientist to propose the expansion of the universe (before Hubble), the majestic evolutionary vision of a Jesuit priest Teilhard de Chardin, we recognise the blurring of lines between the realms of science and religion. The scientist Albert Einstein once wrote that, 'Science without religion is lame and religion without science is blind'.

An encouraging development in the relationships between science and religion is the growing discourse between science and religion in conferences and shared wisdoms. Science and religion have complementary roles to play in the story of the human species and the universe. Science and religion have the potential to work together in mutual understanding for the benefit of everything thing in creation. Both science and religion must learn to respect the different spheres of knowledge, assumptions and methodologies that characterise each discipline. According to Kung, in advocating a complementary approach and constructive interaction between religion and science, he proposes that, *all illegitimate transitions are avoided and all absolutizings are rejected, but in mutual questioning and enrichment people attempt to do justice to reality as a whole in all its dimensions* (41). A complementary and constructive interaction between religion and science will enrich Christian teachings on the origins of the universe and the human species. Such teachings must be in accord with the demonstrated insights of evolutionary science as well as fidelity to the essence of God's revelation. A confrontational approach between science and religion is no longer useful or relevant.

An illustration of the interplay between science and religion is to consider the varying approaches to the interpretation of the Bible, especially the biblical account of creation. During the last 150 years, evolutionary science has generated at least three broad responses to the biblical account of creation.

Creationists are religious fundamentalists who believe in a literal interpretation of the Bible. They uphold the belief that the Bible is God's word and should be understood as written - Adam and Eve were our first parents, the world was created in seven days and so on. The last 200 years of biblical scholarship are rejected or ignored.

Intelligent Design Theory (IDT) is a much more nuanced and complex constellation of theories about the creation story. Those who support some version of IDT would argue for the necessity of an intelligence and design in how the universe operates. Religious opponents of IDT contend that such a position is a kind of nature predestination and limits the creative energy of the Spirit in an evolving universe for the unexpected to happen.

Evolutionary Creation is a third position for Christians who would hold that God is present within the dynamics of creation and also a creative Energy beyond the process of creation. Risk and unpredictability are inherent in the way in which creation happens and evolves. God is not limited by any predetermined plan about the character of creation. God invites humans to share God's intimacy with the wonders of creation.

Understanding emergence

One of the underlying themes in this book is the theme of 'Emergence'. What does the science of Emergence mean? The new science of emergence proposes how evolution happens and how new systems are created from previous subsystems. A simple example to illustrate the meaning of the science of Emergence is the wonder of how water is formed from hydrogen and oxygen. There is nothing in the two elements of hydrogen or oxygen which would lead anyone to predict that water would be formed from the marriage of those two elements (Phipps: 358).

A chemist and Nobel Prize winner (1977) Ilya Prigogine (1917-2003) discovered the process of how life evolves into more complex systems after the original system falls into disorder. Scientific studies show how new elements or properties arise out of properties existing in the system but form different characters. The various components of something emerge sometimes into a new form which is not made up of previous parts (Hubbard 76-78). The theory of Emergence may help us explain how *homo sapiens* emerged from the various dissipative strains of hominids who were the immediate ancestors of humans. According to Phipps, *It (emergence) names the wonderful creativity of our cosmic story- radically new capacities and higher levels of being do emerge in this marvellous universe. And it brings to light realities that have always been important in both theology and science – such as how and why human beings seem to be unique among nature's inhabitants* (Phipps: 357).

The science of emergence has significant implications on how Christianity is being challenged to evolve in its theology and its teachings. How does the glory of Easter emerge from the horrors of Calvary? How do the dissipative elements of betrayal, scourging, crowned with thorns, and excruciating agony of crucifixion become the shining light of Christ risen? Faced with the advent of a second Axial era or new leap in consciousness, Christianity needs to evolve new patterns of thought to capture the spirit and essence of Jesus who became the Christ.

If Christianity in the West seems to be falling into disorder, then the very disorder presents the Christian community with a golden opportunity to constitute a new form of structure for the Christ story. The 'old' pre-scientific religious concepts do not resonate with a new generation of people who are now formed by the world of cyber space, globalisation and new cosmology.

How might the Christ story emerge from the way its basic beliefs have been communicated? According to Ilia Delio, a Religious Sister in the Franciscan order, *in Jesus something new emerges, a new consciousness, a new relatedness, and a new immediacy of God's* presence (2011:55). By trusting in the Spirit of truth to lead the Christian community to an enhanced understanding of God's revelation in Jesus, anxieties about an unknown future will dissipate. Christianity cannot go back to apply past modes of thought as a response to new times.

Conclusion

This chapter has discussed the first six elements in the scaffolding erected related to the central theme of how the Genesis origin myth may be interpreted and appreciated as a story of Emergence and not Fall. Religious stories help people make sense of life mysteries. Higher levels of consciousness empower us to enter more fully into the essence of a religious story. All language about religion is limited in how it expresses the mystery of divinity. In a scientifically formed cultural environment, it is imperative that religions communicate their stories in ways that are credible to the insights of modern science without in any way denying the authenticity of religious experience and integrity of sacred myths. Science and theology should be partners in the search for truth, the betterment of humankind and wellbeing of creation.

The story of the evolution of the universe and humans offers many insights as to how we may appreciate an interpretation of the Genesis origin myth as Emergence and not Fall. In the next chapter, we will consider God's revelation in the story of the universe and human evolution.

CHAPTER THREE

The evolution of the universe and humankind

This chapter first considers two further scaffolding issues: the evolution of the universe and the evolution of the human species. The text then examines how the composition of the Genesis origin myth was told and how it was interpreted as a framework for the Christian story, especially in formulating beliefs about Jesus who became the Christ.

The story of the universe

For a person of religious faith, the story of God and humankind does not begin with God's revelation to the human species but with the amazing story of the evolution of the universe beginning about 13.7 billion years ago. Perhaps about two million years ago, some form of primates appeared; and *Homo sapiens* (wise person) evolved about 120,000 years ago.

The overarching story for all cultures and religious traditions is the story of the universe. A modern narrative of the universe tells of almost limitless spaces, black holes, dark matter, billions of galaxies and stars, chaos and order and the universe expanding into an unknown future. There may be many universes. Our current generation is the first generation to possess a moderate, comprehensive scientific understanding of the extraordinary dimensions of the unfolding universe. However, cosmologists hasten to add that our knowledge of the universe is extremely limited. Scientists believe we know only about 4% of the universe. The other 96% consists of dark matter and dark energy. In 2019 a spacecraft Euclid will begin a mission to study dark energy. Currently we can see only about 3% of the universe. Twenty-three per cent of the universe is dark matter and 74% is dark energy which has a gravitational pull in reverse.

The universe is expanding not contracting, as demonstrated in 1920 by the scientist Edwin Hubble (1889-1953). The universe is expanding at exactly the right speed for new structures to be formed rather than simply collapse. Scientists now believe that they have found one of the keys to understanding the evolution of the universe with the discovery in 2012 of a subatomic particle consistent with the Higgs Boson theory formulated 30 years ago. The 'Higgs field' is a force which permeates the universe and gives particles their mass.

About 13.7 billion years ago, the universe was born. Swimme and Tucker describe the Big Bang as, *all of space and time and mass and energy began as a single point that was trillions of degrees hot and instantly rushed apart* (5). Out of almost nothing came everything that is and has been. Indispensable chemical elements burst forth from the Big Bang and over billions of years gradually emerged into organic life. Our solar system appeared about 4.6 billion years ago. There are at least 100 billion galaxies. The Milky Way, our own galaxy, has 100 billion stars. Scientists have discovered how bacteria found in rock are more than three billion years old. The first Ice Age was 2.3 billon years ago. The earth was positioned at exactly the right distance from the sun for life to flourish. Closer to the sun was too hot for life on earth. Further away from the sun was too cold for life to exist.

Life on earth appeared about one billion years ago and organisms appear in the course of evolutionary history. Multi-cellular animals emerged about 570 million years ago. During the Cambrian period 542-488 million years ago, a rich variety of life forms appeared in the sea. The first vertebrates moved to the land about 375 million years ago. Life became abundant on land during the Triassic (245-206) and Jurassic (206-144) periods with reptiles, mammals and dinosaurs roaming the earth. The extraordinary outburst of life was followed by a period of mass extinctions, known as the Great Dying. About 70% of all animal species became extinct. Dinosaurs evolved about 235 million years ago and became extinct about sixty-five million years ago. About 150 million years ago birds appeared. Flowers appeared about this time and decked the world with their beautiful colours. Grass spread across the lands about twenty-four million years ago. By six million years ago, there were eight thousand species of grass which covered about one quarter of the planet. 400,000 species of plants eventually flourished.

The evolutionary nature of all things in creation is not a theory but a proven fact in science. For a person of religious faith, God is the Divine Energy who initiates the on-going evolution of all life in the universe. In the words of the theologian Paul Tillich, God is the 'Ground of Being', the ultimate Source of all consciousness and life. Evidence from a number of disciplines has confirmed that ecosystems evolved from the primitive communities of simple cells (Edwards 1999:4-7). Life forms evolved from microbes to cells to organisms, vertebrates and ultimately to the human person.

Modern evolutionary world views have their genesis in the works of Charles Darwin (1809-1882), Alfred Russell Wallace (1823-1913) and Jean Baptiste de Lamarck (1774- 1829). Darwin's *On the Origin of Species* (1859) opened a whole new understanding of life in the universe and how people evolved. Darwin's investigations sought to discover answers to two basic questions which emerged from his research: 'How do we make sense of the diversity of life?' and 'How does one species evolve into another species?' Darwin showed how biological life was shaped by natural laws. Since the time of Darwin, there has been considerable debate on the relationship between changes in the genes (mutations) and inherited characteristics through a process of natural selection in evolution.

The story of humankind

Evolutionary theory offers a more scientifically substantiated story about the human species although there are vigorous debates on almost every statement about their origins and dispersion. Our brains clearly show our biological ancestry from reptiles to marsupials to humans. About seven million years ago, an apelike species evolved. The increase in brain size in *Homo habalis* ('handy man'), the first known species of the genus of *Homo*, enabled these creatures to begin to use fire, to run like modern humans and to make stone tools. Primitive humans (*Homo erectus*) evolved about two million years ago although the human species with symbolic consciousness as we know it today is probably only 120,000 years old. By 'symbolic consciousness' we mean how self-reflective thought evolved in *homo sapiens* enabling a person to create, be aware of experiences, to use language and to develop self-identity. Recent, new fossil finds in Kenya by palaeontologists confirm that there are at least two lineages of early humans and the human evolution was, in the words of Professor Spoor, 'clearly not in a straight line'. Fossil records show a strange mix of interbreeding with different species, some of the species which then became extinct thus posing fascinating puzzles for DNA research in human development.

Just over 80,000 years ago, a small group of the *homo sapiens* left North-Eastern Africa, crossed the Red Sea: one group turned north towards Europe, the other travelled east towards India. Over the next 20,000 years, this tiny group multiplied and spread across the globe. Other theories about the evolution of the human species propose origins of some genetic strands of the human species in Siberia and Southeast Asia. An ancient skull found in northern Laos suggests that a modern species of humans had settled in Southeast Asia as early as 60,000 years ago. The Neanderthal species disappeared about 23,000 years ago. Of the possible four types of human species, only one type survived. Adaptability to changing climate conditions seems to be the key to why *homo sapiens* species survived as the only one from a very diverse family tree.

After thousands of years of being wandering hunters, humans began to settle on fertile lands such as the Nile in Africa, the Indus in India, the Yellow river in China and the Tigris in Mesopotamia. Out of those early settlements civilisations began to emerge. Through flexibility with their environment, early humans gradually learned to adapt to new challenges in food gathering and communal living. During the last 10,000 years the temperature of the earth has remained relatively stable, allowing agriculture to spread and civilisations established. In 10,600 BCE settlements were formed in the Middle East.

Wheat and barley began to be cultivated. The cultivation of wheat as a species of grass enabled towns to develop with a food supply close by instead of hunting roaming animals for food. Bread making, stone cutting, wheeled transport and metallurgy helped build these civilisations. The development of bureaucracy, administration and legislation brought order to emerging civilisations.

Through the advent of symbolic consciousness, language developed enabling early humans to externalise their experiences through art, music and story. How and when this dramatic movement in the evolution of the human species occurred is a matter of conjecture among scientists. Did the hominid mind suddenly become aware of the interior life or did the evolution of self consciousness gradually happen over several thousand years, perhaps between 120,000 to sixty thousand years ago? What we do know is that the evolution of self consciousness opened out vast vistas of creativity, language, self-identity, technologies and cultural awareness. When the human species crossed the threshold into self-consciousness, the modern person was born. Writing was invented in Mesopotamia about 5000 years ago. Each succeeding generation could now draw on the wisdoms of previous generations about survival and expanding knowledge.

Evolution and the Christian story

St Anselm (1033-1109) proposed the dictum, *fides quaerens intellectum* (Latin: 'faith seeking understanding') to express the ongoing search for truth through the intersection of faith with life experiences. By our very nature, humans possess an inner energy which drives us onwards to probe the mysteries of life in creation. St Augustine echoed this sentiment by writing, 'Oh God, our hearts are restless until they rest in you'.

The story of an evolutionary creation is the context for religious stories. The character of religion is situated in a time and place of religious consciousness. The first 'religions' were variations of animism which believed spirits in nature were an explanation for everything that happened (Stewart: 28-29). Belief in some form of afterlife has a long history. Neanderthal burial sites reveal remains of food and weaponry that were buried with the dead indicating that these early people believed in some form of afterlife. It is interesting to note how different religions told creation myths from different perspectives. For example, religions of Indian origins (Hinduism, Buddhism) tended to propose a movement towards unity of divine spirits and humans. Myths of Chinese origins such as Confucianism promoted harmony between heaven and earth. Near Eastern origins (Judaism, Christianity, Islam) highlighted opposition between God and sinful creatures and loss of harmony between creator and creation (Kung: 110).

The mystery of evil and suffering is an enduring motif in religious mythologies. Throughout the ages people have wondered about such questions as, *Why do people suffer? What is the meaning of death? Why is there evil in the world? If God or a divine Being is good, why does the divine Being allow evil and suffering?* In the Hebrew Scriptures, the Book of Job addresses these questions without any conclusion except for Job to acknowledge that God's ways are beyond understanding (Job Ch 42).

Religious mythologies express the mystery of evil and suffering in symbolic language. Some mythologies propose a ferocious battle between the forces of good and evil. In ancient Persian philosophy of Manichaeism, the god of good (Ormuzd) engages in endless battles with the god of evil (Ahriman). In the Babylon epic *Atrahasis* (before 1600 BCE), the gods are worn down by the many tasks they have to perform. Eventually they rebel and, *cut the throat of a god with his blood and flesh.* During their time of exile in Babylon, the Jews were greatly influenced by Babylonian mythology. They understood the great battle between good and evil was between God and Satan. Satan was a fallen angel who had disobeyed God and was cast out of God's presence. St Paul also believed evil was an external force (Romans 7:13-17). The Fall myth was composed out of Babylonian origin myths.

Before we have a closer look at the Fall myth in Genesis, it is noted that Genesis 1-3 is actually two different stories of creation, separated by at least 500 years. Scripture scholars suggest that Genesis 1 to 2:4a was composed by the so called 'priestly' writers' during the Babylonian exile. This text in sixth century BCE described creation as good and living harmoniously in the garden. Possibly the famous Babylon gardens provided an image of the Eden garden. Resting on the Sabbath is given a particular emphasis to give the exiled Jewish people identity among the Babylonians.

The second account of creation is called the 'Yahwist' source because it uses the name *Yahweh* for God. This account was composed perhaps 400 to 500 years earlier, perhaps during the reign of King Solomon. The 'Yahwist' source offers a primitive story where man is made of dust, woman is subordinate to man and Adam and Eve are expelled from the garden for disobeying God. The act of disobedience and expulsion from the garden became known in Christian theology as the Fall. According to the myth, God meted out severe punishments for this act of defiance. God condemned Adam and Eve to experience death, suffer pain in childbirth and toil for their living in an unforgiving earth (Genesis 3:14-19).

The traditional interpretation of the Fall myth became deeply imbedded in how Christians understood suffering, sin and evil. Folklore, household stories, liturgical prayer, cartoons, art, dramatic presentations, cultural symbols and time honoured sayings all conspired to affirm the image of Adam and Eve in the paradise garden and their consequent disgrace. Misogynist 'jokes' abound about Adam and Eve and the forbidden fruit, e.g. 'Just look what the first woman Eve did to us by convincing Adam to eat the fruit!' and so on. Consider how a friend of mine recently responded to our conversation about a newspaper report which described an appalling massacre of innocent people. My friend said, 'Yes, this massacre is indeed a shocking thing to happen. Why is there such evil in the world? What a tragedy! If only things had turned out differently at the beginning of our existence and our first parents had not disobeyed God!' Then he added with a rueful laugh, only half serious, 'Adam and Eve have a lot to answer for, don't they?'

In the New Testament writings, the Fall myth offered an appropriate context for understanding the meaning of the death of Jesus. This topic will be discussed later in the text. Questions such as the following arise from a reflection on the Genesis origin myth:

- What if there was no Fall in the literalist mode of interpreting the origin myth in Genesis?

- If there was no traditional interpretation of the Fall, how might the Jesus the Christ story be told in the light of modern science and cosmology?

- Is it possible for Christians to compose a New Story which is in continuity with the deepest traditions in Christology and yet resonates with contemporary consciousness?

To respond to these questions, it is helpful to begin with a review of how main elements of the traditional Christian story were told over the 2000 years.

Traditional story for Christians

In the traditional story of how the Fall myth was interpreted, the narrative is told in the following sequence:

God created the world.

God created human beings, Adam and Eve, who lived in the Garden of Eden.

Everything was harmonious in the garden.

God commanded Adam and Eve not to eat the fruit from the Tree of Knowledge of good and evil.

Adam and Eve were tempted by Satan and they ate the forbidden fruit.

God punished Adam and Eve for their disobedience and they were driven out of the garden of Paradise.

Adam and Eve and their descendents were condemned to endure hardships.

The act of disobedience and expulsion from Paradise is known as the Fall. Later in the development of Christian doctrine, the teachings about Original Sin became part of Christian corpus of beliefs.

The *Catechism of the Catholic Church* (1994) is quite explicit in explaining the significance of the Fall for Christian teachings:

The account of the Fall in Genesis 3 uses figurative language but affirms a primeval event, a deed that took place at the beginning of the history of man. Revelation gives us the certainty of faith that the whole of human history is marked by the original fault freely committed by our first parents (390).

The harmony in which they found themselves, thanks to original justice, is now destroyed: the control of the soul's faculties over the body is shattered; the union of man and woman becomes subject to tensions, their relations henceforth marked by lust and domination. Harmony with creation is broken: visible creation has become alien and hostile to man,...(400).

But we do know by revelation that Adam had received original holiness and justice not for himself alone, but for all human nature. By yielding to the tempter, Adam and Eve committed a personal sin but this sin affected the human nature that they would then transmit in a fallen state (404).

The coming of Christ

Within the Fall tradition, a dominant Christology was taught throughout the Christian story as follows:

Many thousands of years after the Fall, God sent his Son Jesus to restore relationships between God and humanity. Jesus suffered and died on the cross as an act of reconciliation with God.

By his act of sacrifice on Calvary, Jesus died to atone for the sins of humankind. His death was a sacrificial act of redemption.

The gates of heaven were opened by the sacrifice of Jesus on Calvary.

Jesus was raised by God as the Christ in the resurrection.

The Christian community continues to celebrate the redemptive mission of Christ.

Christ is the Saviour of the world.

Those who are fortunate to be baptised have their sins washed away by the waters of Baptism.

The *Catechism of the Catholic Church* explains the role of Christ in salvation history, linking Christ's death on the cross with the consequences of the Fall:

The Christian tradition sees in this passage an announcement of a 'New Adam' who, because he 'became obedient unto death, even death on the cross', makes amends superabundantly for the disobedience of Adam (411).

The Council of Trent (1545- 1563) reaffirmed the doctrine of Christ's redemptive action as an act of reparation for the primal sin of Adam and Eve.

We know that there was no such person as a physical 'Adam' or a physical 'Eve'. In Hebrew the names mean Mr Creature and Mrs Life. The names are symbolic names representing the first human beings and all humanity. The name 'Adam' is a generic name meaning in Hebrew (*adama*) 'earth creature'.

To save Christians from scientific ridicule, Christians must move from any vestiges of literalism in pre-scientific age mythology and reconstruct their essential story in narratives that are aligned with the best of modern science while preserving the religious meaning of myths within their tradition. Biblical assumptions about the three tiered nature of the universe (heavens, earth and the underworld), multiplication of loaves and fishes, Jesus walking on water, sun standing still, 'descent into hell', ascending to heaven, a fig tree withering after a curse, demons crying out, are examples of biblical literature which are to be reinterpreted in the light of modern science and mythology.

We are not suggesting that the mystical elements of religion should be reduced to pragmatic science research or scientific methodology. Science is always a 'work in progress'. Apart from the changing face of science, science cannot explain issues relating to the meaning of life such as love and compassion. The religious world is as real as the scientific world but begins with different assumptions about reality. Religion seeks to explain the meaning and purpose of life. Religion has to utilise symbolic language and imagination to express the transcendent mystery of divinity.

For almost 2000 years, a literal reading of the biblical account of creation was taken as a given. Modern science has eroded any literal interpretation of the creation story. The Bible must be read from the perspective and assumptions of the symbolism of sacred myths. The Noah flood story in Genesis (Ch7) is an insightful symbolic story about fidelity to God and the cosmic consequences of sin. Taken literally, the story is scientifically absurd. How could water cover the whole earth and when the flood subsided where did all the water go from the flooded earth? Biblical images have to be deconstructed and reconstructed to resonate with contemporary scientific consciousness without, however, trying to frame the symbols into scientific assumptions about the nature of reality. A failure to reconcile the Christ story with the best of modern science will consign Christianity to intellectual wilderness. God is truth and Christians must be courageous in their faith quest for truth. An authentic church is a truthful church.

Given the different assumptions and methodology of science and religion, there will always be some healthy tension between them. A false syncretism is to be avoided. The history of the relationships between religion and science would send out a warning to those theologians who would hitch their theology to the latest scientific chariot. Because scientific theories come and go, theology would be left red faced when the latest scientific was discredited.

The failure of Christianity generally to respond creatively to the advent of modern science in the 19th century and until the second phase of the 20th century left Christianity weakened to impart the wisdom of the gospel into the public arena. The loss for science is a weakened propensity to offer ethical foundations for its research. Even today, about 40% of Christians in USA believe a literal interpretation of the Genesis story. Forty-eight per cent of Christians in USA believe Christ will return within the next forty years.

The New Atheism, exemplified by the biologist Richard Dawkins (*The God Delusion* 2006), Daniel Dennett (*Breaking the Spell* 2007) and Christopher Hitchens (*God is not Great* 2009) pours scorn on some anti-scientific Christian teachings. While it is easy to dismiss such writers as ill-informed about the nature of religion and almost totally ignorant of contemporary biblical scholarship and current science-religious dialogue, their very popularity in the public domain is a wake-up call for Christians to get their belief house in credible order and communicate it effectively. A popular assumption in the media is that being a religious believer, and at the same time being comfortable with modern science, are irreconcilable positions to uphold. There is a long list of eminent scientists who were also committed Christians - Mendel, Pasteur, Le Maitre, Teilhard de Chardin and Polkinghorne, to name a few.

Conclusion

This chapter has explored two further scaffolding issues in the exploration of the Genesis origin myth: the story of the universe and the evolution of the human species. The universe story is a narrative of explosions of creative energy, chaos, disintegration, new births, extinctions, Ice Ages and Warm Ages, life emerging out of oceans and a full flowering of an amazing diversity of life forms in the web of life in creation. Tribal groups and civilisations composed sacred stories to make sense of life mysteries, especially the mystery of suffering and death. One such sacred story is the Genesis origin story which is a key dimension in God's revelation to humankind.

The following chapter will consider the Genesis origin myth and examine how its traditional interpretation has shaped the Christian story.

CHAPTER FOUR

Traditional interpretations of the Genesis story

This chapter discusses the Genesis origin story of the Fall and examines questions arising from a traditional literal interpretation of the sacred myth, including how the doctrine of original sin became part of the corpus of Christian doctrine. Other issues associated with the Fall tradition, such as the Fall and creation, the Fall and death, pessimistic spirituality, dualism and negative anthropology were the fruits of biblical literalism and dualistic philosophies.

Anticipated criticisms of the theme of the book

At this point, I need to divert briefly from the theme of this chapter to comment on anticipated criticisms of the thesis of the book.

A much repeated criticism of the theme of this book is that the whole topic is very much a 'use-by-date' topic. Critics complain, 'Why all the fuss about the Fall story? Even as a child we were told that the story was a symbolic story about the presence of sin in the world'. Another comment from some theologians is that the topic has been around for many years and modern theology has moved well beyond the topic. While these comments may have some validity, the theological and pastoral reality at grassroots level of liturgy, devotional prayer and catechesis reflect a more traditional interpretation of the origin myth.

Discourse in the secure and comfortable theological corridors about the Fall may well be passé but my observation is that public teachings in seminaries and official church centres are very different propositions. Also, I have yet to see evidence that the specific teachings in the *Catechism of the Catholic Church* on this topic are heralded for forthcoming revision. When has the reader attended officially sponsored church theological conferences where the topic of Christianity within an evolutionary paradigm has been openly discussed and received public ecclesial affirmation?

Reflections on the fall story

The Genesis origin myth Chapter 2-3 has traditionally been interpreted as a Fall. Let us reflect on its text and then comment on the elements of the story.

In the following reflections, I am indebted to the insights of Harold K Kushner in his book, *How good do we have to be? A new understanding of guilt and forgiveness*. Because the Genesis story has often been interpreted literally and its literalism has shaped Christian theology and anthropology, I will comment on the aspect of literalism in how the myth was traditionally interpreted.

Consider the following observations about the Fall story.

If the Tree of Knowledge of Good and Evil was about making a moral choice and Adam and Eve had no such prior gift of moral choice, how were they able to make a moral choice to obey or not obey God's command?

What does the story say about the image of God who severely punished, not only Adam and Eve, but all humankind for a single act of disobedience? Does not God's action seem extreme or even bizarre? Why does God not offer a simple gesture of forgiveness rather than punish the whole human race for all time? Is God really a capricious deity holding lasting grudges against humanity? Collective or group punishment used to be accepted in past times. The Geneva Convention in 1949 declared group punishment a war crime.

The Fall story has no mention of sin. In Chapter 4, when Cain kills his brother Abel, then indeed sin is committed. Notice also the first sin in the Cain and Abel story is not against God but a destruction of human relationships by a brutal murder. As stated earlier in the book, the Adam and Eve myth is never referred to in the Hebrew scripture as the Fall. The term 'Fall' is a theological not a biblical term. The Fall tradition became so imbedded into the Christian story that its traditional interpretation generated a dominant Christology. Such was the character of the Christology that it utilised the Fall as a lens from which Christian theology understood the mission of Christ.

How congruent is the Fall story with the findings in anthropology about the evolution of the human species throughout millions of years from a single cell to cellular complexity? There are spirited debates among palaeontologists about our human origins. Humans evolved from the great apes to *Homo erectus* (upright humans) during the last two million years. Modern humans are about 120,000 years old. East Africa has been identified as a major fountainhead for the dispersal of the human species as has been previously mentioned in the book. Other hypotheses about human origins are discussed elsewhere.

Monogenesis (one origin of the human race) is not generally accepted by the majority of science. Anthropologists in their DNA studies have reached a general consensus that monogenesis cannot be scientifically substantiated. Humans gradually evolved from different strands of life, probably from two or even from four strands of life. One strand of *Homo genus*, the Neanderthal, became extinct about 23,000 years ago. Human beings evolved from different pairs of primates in different geographical settings over millions of years. In genetic studies, some anthropologists propose that the primal 'Adam' was separated from the primal 'Eve' by about 90,000 years (Flannery: 74). If palaeontologists are correct in their consensus about polygenesis (from many couples), how would all humankind inherit the consequences of the Fall if only one couple disobeyed God?

In a traditional Christian interpretation of the fall, what questions arise for the Christian story?

Does the coming of Jesus as the Christ suggest that Christ was an after-thought of God's plan for creation? In other words, if the original Plan A failed, then Plan B was ready to swing into action as a back-up measure to rectify the situation and restore humanity to God's favour. Are Christians really required to accept Plan B which said that God locked everybody that has been born out of heaven until Jesus died to open up the gates of paradise?

Surely a loving God did not and would not require his Son to endure horrific sufferings in the crucifixion as some kind of restitution for a purported act of disobedience committed in the mists of history.

If redemption of humanity's sinfulness was the primary purpose of Jesus, then the centrality of the Christ story would be focused on the last few hours of Jesus in his suffering and death rather than his whole teaching mission for the reign of God and 'life in abundance' (John 10:10).

The fall and original sin

What anthropological evidence is there for the doctrine of original sin which became official Catholic teaching after the fifth century? Does not human experience tells us that we are born both blessed and broken into a morally ambivalent world? Neither the scriptures, nor early church teachings, Orthodox Christianity, Judaism and Islam support a notion of original sin as inherited by each individual person. Rather, these traditions teach about sin as a mysterious flawed human condition.

St Paul wrote about sin entering the world through the disobedience of Adam and Eve, *Therefore, just as sin came into the world through one man, and death came through sin, and so death spread to all because all have sinned* (Romans 5:12). Paul never explained how the first sin was transmitted to humanity. Paul wrote how the first sin had left sinful desires or concupiscence in the hearts of all people, *but I am of the flesh, sold into slavery under sin. For I do not understand my own actions. For I do not do what I want, but I do the very thing I hate* (Romans 7: 14-15).

The term 'original sin' is a creation of Augustine. In later years, Augustine was overwhelmed by depression at the sight of civilisation crumbling before his very eyes with barbarian tribes pouring across the frontiers of the Roman Empire, plundering all in their path. Augustine believed that God had condemned much of humanity to eternal damnation because of Adam's sin. He wrote, *banished (from Paradise) after his sin Adam bound his offspring also with the penalty of death and damnation... So the matter stood; the damned lump of humanity was lying prostrate, no, it was wallowing in evil* (Enchyridion 26.27).

Scholars suggest that Augustine used a faulty Old Latin translation of the Greek text in Romans 5:12. The Greek text from Paul's letter stated 'since when all have sinned'. Augustine and his contemporaries translated that statement as 'in Adam', indicating that because of Adam's sin, everyone born inherits the first (original) sin (Maloney: 52-53). From this time onwards, Western Christianity, following Augustine, taught that we all begin life as alienated sinners or in Augustine's words as *massa damnata*. The doctrine of original sin was declared and defined at the Councils of Carthage (418), Orange (529) and Trent (1546). The Council of Trent taught that Adam's original sin was transmitted by propagation from generation to generation. In other words, original sin was transmitted by intercourse. The *Catechism of the Catholic Church* further extended the doctrine of original sin by teaching how Adam and Eve's sin affected human nature which had been deprived of the original innocence of Adam and Eve (no. 404).

Perhaps at a later date, church historians will satisfactorily explain why the official Western church (in contrast to the Orthodox church) adopted Augustine's extreme pessimism about humanity, a position which stands at variance to the Incarnation and the life and teachings of Jesus. I surmise that the high esteem of Augustine held by theologians generated a 'halo' effect on his writings. Another factor was the strong influence of Gnosticism in the first centuries of Christianity. The Gnostics believed that matter was evil and a prison for the soul. The body therefore was corrupt. Body was bad, soul was good. Manichaeism was a later form of Gnosticism and held a similar position about the dualism within a human person. Augustine belonged to the Manichaeism sect for eight years although later in life he denounced Manichaeism. Augustine's personal struggle with sexuality and chastity shaped his writings on sin. (Toews: 78 - 89)

A further issue in Augustine's position was his struggle against a British monk Pelagius (c 390-418) who purportedly taught that individuals could achieve salvation without the need of God's grace. Augustine's writings and preaching against Pelagius led him to combat the perceived optimism of Pelagius by adopting the opposite extreme with a very pessimistic view of humanity.

Scholars now acknowledge that Augustine and his supporters misunderstood the theological position of Pelagius but that topic belongs to another book.

Belief about original sin led to the concept of Limbo. Limbo was designated as a place where unbaptised children go after they die. With the spread of teachings about original sin, Baptism began to be viewed, not only as a sacrament of initiation into the Christian community, but a necessary condition for salvation. Therefore, children who died before being baptised went to Limbo. They could not enter heaven because they were not baptised. They could not merit punishment in hell so theologians had to construct another place for their destiny which they called 'Limbo'. The tradition of baptising dying babies persisted until the last fifty years. Even as a child, I heard stories of Catholic nurses baptising babies in danger of death.

The problem of misinterpreting the Genesis story was compounded through the writings of the most influential theologian in Christian history, Thomas Aquinas. Thomas and his fellow Dominicans understood the Messiah as fulfilling God's promise to send a redeemer to rectify the disobedience of Adam and Eve. Therefore, the motivation for the incarnation was redemption of the human race from inherited sinfulness. The Council of Trent (1545-1563) affirmed the belief that the mission of Jesus was to atone for the first sin of Adam and Eve. Scholastic atonement theology dominated the Catholic theological landscape until well into the 20th century. Reformation theology was strongly focused on redemption theology, especially in the works of Martin Luther and John Calvin. The Franciscans proposed another motive for the incarnation. A Franciscan, Duns Scotus (14th century), proposed that love was the driving energy for the incarnation.

It is interesting to observe some congruence between the notion of Emergence rather than Fall with the work of St Irenaeus of Lyons (d 202). St Irenaeus, one of the most eminent of the early Church Fathers, proposed that the incarnation would have happened, irrespective of whether Adam and Eve had sinned. Their sin had tarnished the 'likeness' of God in humanity. Christ's action was not only to restore this 'likeness', but bring humanity to a new wholeness in a wonderful relationship with God. The incarnation was intended by God, *as a plan for the fullness of time, to gather up all things in him, things in heaven and things on earth* (Ephesians 1:9-10).

In the New Testament, there were diverse motives offered to explain the mission of Jesus. These motives will be discussed in the next chapter.

The fall and creation

A further issue arising from an interpretation of the Genesis myth as Fall is the implication that the unfolding story of the universe is irrelevant to the Christ story except as a backdrop or stage setting to the salvation story. Is the story about the billions of years of the evolving universe divorced from the story of human kind and the incarnation? What does the neglect of situating the Fall story within creation assume about beliefs concerning creation as the primal revelation of God?

A literal interpretation of the Fall story highlighted humans as alienated *from* creation, not in affinity **with** creation. Adam and Eve were driven out of the garden. Does not the 'exile' motif suggest disengagement from creation rather than partnership with creation? The biblical image for the human species is both 'breath of God' and 'earth' (Genesis 2: 7). In the words of Adrian Smith, *we humans are not separate beings on earth but rather expressions of earth* (2011:72).

In contrast to the 'exile' motif in the Fall story, it should be noted that in the later story of creation, the 'priestly' account (Genesis 1-2:4a), creation is celebrated as good, *God saw everything that he had made and indeed it was very good* (Genesis 1:31). God is a mysterious Energy whose presence infuses the whole of creation. God is never absent or disconnected from the world. The Divine Energy or Spirit creates and sustains all things in creation. In the Bible, there are numerous nature images of God such as Rock (1 Corinthians 10:4), Water (Revelations 22:1), Fire (Deuteronomy 1:33), Light (1 John 1:5). Theologians describe God's relationship with the world as 'panentheism', meaning God is in the world and is also beyond the world. Our very existence, our life, our oxygen and our food are utterly dependent on the energies of the Spirit within the network of life. For a person of religious faith, God is first known in and through creation. Creation may be described as a manifestation of the self-giving or altruism of God's love.

The fall and death

Death did not come as a consequence of a primal act of disobedience. In the interpretation of the Fall tradition, death is punishment for sin (Genesis 2:17). St Paul reiterated this Jewish belief (Romans 6:23). Our knowledge of the dynamics of the universe highlights the violence of the evolutionary process of the universe story as well as its beauty. The experience of death is an integral feature of everything in creation. In the process of evolution, there are winners and losers in survival or extinction. Stars explode or are blasted away by stellar collisions. Lions hunt and kill gazelles. Whales swallow small fish.

Eagles swoop from the sky to pluck up tiny lambs. Millions of years before humans emerged, plants, trees, animals, fish, birds lived and died.

Extinction of species is part of the evolutionary pattern of life. Throughout the history of the earth, there have been five major mass extinctions of life resulting from dramatic changes. For example about 250 million years ago there was a massive extinction of life, as many as 90% of marine life and 65% of earth's species perished in the close of the Permian period. As recently as 74,000 years ago, a violent volcanic explosion in Sumatra (Indonesia) poured a deadly volcanic cloud into the sky wiping out most species with perhaps only a few thousand species surviving the freezing cold. After periods of mass extinctions, it takes millions of years for new extensive life forms to evolve.

The fall and women

By blaming the woman Eve for the Fall, patriarchy (Father rule) was reinforced. From the writings of the Church Fathers, we read how the symbolic woman Eve was demonised by some Church Fathers as the one who caused the Fall by tempting Adam. The letters of Jerome (d 420) are replete with comments which castigated women as evil temptresses and an ever present danger to humankind. Tertullian (d c 200), one of the prominent Church Fathers, in his book, *On the apparel of women* wrote:

You are the devil's gateway; you are the unsealer of that forbidden tree; you are the first deserter of the divine law; you are she who persuaded him whom the devil was not valiant enough to attack. You destroyed so easily God's image, man. On account of your desertion even the son of God had to die. (Vol. IV of *The Anti-Nicene Fathers*. Grand Rapids. Mi. Wm. B. Eerdmans. 1975 1:1).

St Ambrose (375) wrote:

We know that Adam did not sin before the woman was created; indeed, after the woman was made, she was the first to violate the divine command. She even dragged her husband along with her into sin and showed herself to be an incentive to him. (*On paradise*, 10, 47).

In the patristic misogynistic tradition, Eve is portrayed as cursed in the pain of giving birth to children rather than blessed for being a mother. Church Fathers such as Justin Martyr (c 160), Irenaeus (130-202) and Tertullian (d c 200), contrasted the obedient Mary with the disobedient Eve, the unbelief of Eve with the faith of Mary. The subordination of women throughout the ages and the dominance of the patriarchal system in Church structures and ministry were reinforced by the Eve syndrome.

In the Genesis myth, Adam was the first creation. Eve was formed from 'the rib of Adam' (Genesis 2:22). According to the myth, Satan knew that the woman Eve was the weak one. Hence Satan tempted her first and it was Eve who was punished by suffering pain in giving birth to children. Describing the denigration of women as a consequence of the Fall, the religious historian Karen Armstrong writes, *Nowhere is this alienation more evident than in the denigration of sexuality and women in particular. Even though Christianity had originally been quite positive for women, it had already developed a misogynistic tendency in the West by the time of Augustine* (1999:149).

When we consider the role of Eve in the Genesis origin myth from the perspective of Emergence not Fall, we may consider that it was Eve who was the courageous one. She was the curious one who took the first step into the unknown by taking the fruit from the Tree of Knowledge, thus entering the brave new but complex world of human existence. Eve is the original pathfinder of the human journey of enlightenment.

The fall and universal redemption

According to the interpretation of the Fall myth, all humankind was morally marked by the disobedience of Adam and Eve. Christian beliefs hold that Jesus came to redeem everybody from an inherently sinful state. However, since Christianity is only 2000 years old and Christians comprise just over 30% of the world's seven billion people, what does it mean to say that 'Jesus died for the sins of humankind' or 'Jesus is Saviour of the world?' According to this belief, those figures suggest that a whole lot of people before the time of Christ, now and in the future, are missing out on God's redemptive plan through Jesus. Does the Christian claim of Christ's redemptive universal mission appear to be rather presumptuous for those of other religious persuasions? One can only wonder what a devout Muslim, Buddhist, Jew or Hindu would make of the Christian belief of universal redemption through Christ?

The great theologian Karl Rahner (d 1984) tried hard to reconcile this dilemma by naming non-Christians as 'anonymous Christians'. Non-Christians were less than impressed by being named as 'anonymous Christians'. How does a religious narrative based on the Fall stand in relationship to an ecumenical perspective on religiosity and spirituality?

Later in the book there will be a discussion of the notion of the Cosmic or Universal Christ which may offer a possible point of reconciliation between the diverse religious traditions and universal redemption.

The fall and pessimistic spirituality

The Fall has shaped a Christian understanding of the human person. The Fall tradition and later the doctrine of original sin taught that we begin life tainted with the sin of Adam and Eve; in other words, we begin life, not in original grace, but in a state of alienation from God and carry an inclination to sin (concupiscence). From birth onwards we must spend our lives overcoming this obsessive guilt and sense of unworthiness. For Christians, the sacrifice of Jesus as the Christ, restored people in God's favour and opened the gates of heaven for salvation. What about the rest of humanity in the saving act of redemption? 'Salvation' was commonly understood as doing enough good deeds to earn grace to attain heaven rather than fostering 'life in abundance' to self, others and creation. The English word 'salvation' traces its origins in Sanskrit, Hebrew, Greek and Latin to words associated with 'healing', 'making one whole' 'to be freed from confinement' and 'regeneration'. In Christianity, 'salvation' was traditionally associated with what happened **after** death if one leads a good life. To verify this observation, a study of Christian spirituality reveals how often the theme of 'wretched sinner', 'unworthiness' and 'sinfulness' appears in the writings of the saints (Freeman: 302).

For most of the history of Christian spirituality, an enduring theme was a rejection of earthly things. Our existence on earth was regarded as a time of testing to see if we were worthy of heaven. Consider the words of the very influential classic, *The Imitation of Christ* (Thomas a Kempis 15th century) which was read by Religious regularly for hundreds of years:

A life of wretchedness, that's what our life on earth is. The higher a man's spiritual aims, the more distasteful does our present life appear to him; he sees more clearly, feels more deeply, the disabilities of our fallen nature (55).

The *Didache*, one of the earliest known Christian pastoral documents of the first or second century, devotes much of the first six chapters to warnings about sins.

The horror of the Black Death (1348-1356) in which about one third of Europe's population died from the plague, reinforced the view that the earth is indeed a hostile place. The Stations of the Cross, which followed the torturous path of Jesus to Calvary, originated as a devotion from this time and is portrayed in every Catholic Church.

In the popular Marian prayer 'Salve Regina' or 'Hail Holy Queen' (11th century) people pray:

'poor banished children of Eve...
mourning and weeping in this valley of tears'.

A verse in the hymn of the eminent Evangelical preacher John Wesley said:

'Strangers and pilgrims here below.
The earth we know is not our place;
and hasten through this vale of woe;
and restless to behold your face'.

Given the harsh living conditions of most people in these times, having to endure periodic famines, plagues and local wars, we can readily appreciate the longing of people for the hope of a better life in heaven. The ancient prayer to the Holy Spirit, ' Veni Sancte Spiritus' includes the verse:

'If you take your grace away,
nothing pure in man (*sic*) will stay'.

The popular hymn 'Praise to the holiest in the height' has the verse:

'O loving wisdom of our God!
When all was sin and shame,
A second Adam to the fight
And to the rescue came.'

On a personal note, consider the following night prayer taught to us children by our parents. Each night before we went to bed, my four brothers and I would kneel by the bed, cross our arms across our chests and recite:

'I must die, I do not know when or where or how,
But if I die in mortal sin,
My soul is lost forever'.

As a family we said the Rosary each night and each decade of the Rosary was concluded by the prayer,

'Oh my God, forgive us our sins,
save us from the fires of hell
and bring all the souls to heaven,
especially those in most need of thy mercy'.

As a child attending the parish mission in a tiny country church, I recall with dread the preacher's fiery talks on hell, especially the images he evoked describing the individual burning pain inflicted by the God of judgment according to the nature of the offense against God. For example, those who drink excessively have an eternal fire burning on their tongues. Because a loved one had recently died from alcohol addiction, tears flowed freely that night in our farm house after returning home from the mission preaching on hell. My father had to lead the burial service of the loved one because, according to canon law at that time, one who died of alcoholism may not have a Catholic burial. Canon law (1917-1981) following the Council of Trent, gave every pastor the right to refuse burial to anyone considered 'a scandal to the church'. Those who scandalised included atheists, blasphemers, alcoholics, those who suicided, those living together in a non- married state and so on.

Evoking the terror of hell has a long history in Christian teaching. Three of the most influential theologians in Christian writings - Augustine, Peter Lombard and Aquinas - all emphasised that the trauma of hell was not only spiritual and mental but physical. Medieval preachers put the number saved from hell as one in 1,000 or even one in 10,000. St Alphonsus Ligouri, the founder of the Redemptorists, published in 1758 *The Eternal Truths* which provided a handy resource for sermons in parishes on hell. One of Reverend Joseph Furniss's children's books *The Sight of Hell* (1882) described how children in hell suffer, 'the little child is in the red hot oven. Hear how it screams to come out... it beats its head against the roof of the oven' (quoted in Johnson: 310). Four million copies of books for children by Furniss were sold in English speaking countries.

I acknowledge that generalisations from personal experiences have very limited universal application. However, research on the history of Christian spirituality would generally support the bias of a guilt orientation in people's relationships with God. The roots of Christian spirituality evolved from Judaism. A key element of the books of the Hebrew scripture was the people's sinfulness before Yahweh. We might even suggest that the Hebrew scripture was obsessed by the consequences of sin. This unhealthy heritage became imbedded into the character of Christian spirituality. Fr Emmett Coyne's book *The Theology of Fear* (2012 published by Create Space) describes his priestly formation which was dominated by the negativity of mortal sins, hell and absolute obedience to the hierarchy.

One needs to avoid overstating the dominance of negativity in the story of Christian spirituality. There are many examples of writings about God's tender mercy, especially in mystics such as Hildegard of Bingen (1098-1179), Julian of Norwich (1342-c 1417), Teresa of Avila (1515-1582) and Meister Eckhart (1260-c1327). The icon of the Sacred Heart, as a counter to the pessimism of Jansenism, became popular in Catholic households after the 17th century. The icon showed the heart of Jesus burning with love and compassion. The much loved statues and images of Mary offered an icon of tenderness and motherly care. Franciscan spirituality was more positive about God's mercy and love for all creatures than the negativity of a Fall orientated spirituality. However, it would not be an exaggeration to propose that the theme of God's mercy tended to be marginalised by the dominance of a guilt/punishment in much of Christian spirituality.

Dualism

Dualism (from the Latin *duo* meaning 'two') refers to the various philosophical beliefs about the two levels of existence in the human person: the physical or bodily and the spiritual.

Matter and spirit are in essential oneness within the human person. There are not two realms of body and spirit within a person, separate from each other. However, the separation of body from spirit has been an enduring cancer in the history of Christian spirituality and spirituality generally. An anti-world bias has been and still is a feature of many spiritual traditions. Both Hinduism and Buddhism advocate an enlightenment which liberates the soul from the bondage of material things and the cycle of birth and death.

When Augustine's interpretation of the Fall evolved into the doctrine of original sin, this doctrine became accepted as orthodox Catholic teaching. The doctrine of original sin was reinforced by the Council of Trent thus firmly supporting the concept of dualism. In a dualistic vision, matter is bad, spirit is good. The body is associated with sinful urges (concupiscence) as opposed to the purity of the soul. Much of early Christianity was influenced by various dualistic philosophies such as Gnosticism, Manichaeism and Neo-Platonic thinking. Dualism was a contradiction of the gift of oneness in the universe with all its blessings of life. Augustine's concept of the 'Two Cities', the *Civitas Dei* (City of God) and *Civitas Terena* (City of the world) envisaged this dualism within the public realm (Bourke 207-219). The tension between the 'Two Cities' continues in contemporary church life. Even today some church teachings reflect a reluctance to engage fully into bringing the gospel into the dynamics of world events and insights from the social sciences. There is a whiff of dualism in the revised liturgy of 2011. Instead of the previous response 'and with you', the revised liturgy now requires the congregation to say 'and with your spirit'. Why not, 'The Lord be with you'?- you, the whole person, you, with your joys and sorrows, your family and life challenges, not just your spirit?

Dualism is a toxic mix in the church's teachings on anthropology and especially teachings on sexuality. Research on people's attitudes to the Church's teachings on sexuality show how few are guided by official church teachings on sexuality. The official teaching church steadfastly refuses to expand natural law thinking on teachings about sexuality to embrace the insights of holistic current theological/psychological thinking relating to such matters as masturbation, contraception and homosexuality.

For more than fifty years, papal teachings on marriage and sexual morality have been defended and those moral theologians questioning the official teachings have been punished and excluded. The church has only itself to blame if it perceives that its teachings are not respected in the rough and tumble of public debates on issues relating to sexuality and marriage. There is an urgent need for those formulating moral teachings to revise church teachings which better reflect the complexity of life situations in the lives of people and the evolutionary nature of our humanity. To fail to do so will marginalise the church even further as an authentic moral teacher for the wider morally diverse society.

Prescriptions in Christian beliefs

It is something of a paradox that, through politics, Christian orthodoxy and loyalty became linked with obedience to specific beliefs rather than a commitment to a way of life. Other great religious traditions, such as Judaism, Islam and Confucian religiosity, all emphasise a **way_**of living. The practice of the 'eightfold path' is a central tenet of Buddhism. Religion is about a transformation of one's life, not primarily about knowing the right theological terminology.

During the era of the Roman Emperor Constantine and succeeding Emperors in the fourth and fifth centuries, upholding the right beliefs in the creed was judged necessary for political unity. The fourth century was a turning point in the history of Christian theology. Christianity was endorsed by the Roman/Byzantine Empire and doctrine fell under state control. The Council of Nicea (325) was summoned by the Emperor, not by the pope. More emphasis began to be placed on what people were required to believe rather than their relationships with God. In reacting to the threat of the Gnostics (*gnosis* Greek: 'inner knowledge'), dogma was linked with right beliefs. Early Church Fathers such as Clement of Alexandria (d 215) held that knowledge of the faith is sufficient for salvation although through faith, one can achieve a higher form of knowledge. In canon law, faith became more an object of the intellect rather than an inner conversion of the heart. Christian spirituality is not about simply following a system of dogmas but fidelity to a way of holistic living in Christ.

According to Freeman, under the Roman Empire, fidelity to orthodoxy was upheld as a political imperative rather than an issue for theological concerns (301). In retrospect, one might argue that the debates between Augustine and Pelagius about the nature of a person and inherited sinfulness needed more time for discernment about the authenticity of the concept of original sin. The debates were eventually stifled for political expediency. The growing halo on Augustine's writings tended to inhibit a serious critique of his writings on original sin, especially when his teaching was affirmed by church councils especially the Council of Trent (1545- 1563) as official Catholic doctrine.

By reinforcing the teachings as stated in the *Catechism of the Catholic Church* concerning a literal understanding of the human species and the doctrine of original sin, the official Church has created a dilemma for ordinary Christians. How does the *magisterium* now modify its teachings in the light of evolutionary science and yet insist its core teachings never change? The *Catechism of the Catholic Church* understood the dilemma when it stated, *The Church knows very well that we cannot tamper with the revelation of original sin without undermining the mystery of Christ* (n 389).

There are several levels of teachings in the church with its hierarchy of truths. However, a commonly expressed mantra, 'church teachings never change' is not only contradicted by numerous examples in history where church teachings have changed, but the mantra flies in the face of how different historical periods generate new levels of consciousness about life generally and theology in particular.

An example of how this mantra of 'church teachings never change' influenced church teachings, is the argument Cardinal Ottaviani used to convince Pope Paul VI not to change church teaching on aspects of sexuality, including contraception, lest it would erode the papal authority of Pius XI in his encyclical *Casti Connubii* (1930). Even though fifty-seven out of the sixty-one delegates in the papal commission advocated some change in the church's position on aspects of sexuality, *Humanae Vitae* was proclaimed in 1968. The encyclical (HV) was a watershed in how people accepted or ignored church teachings, especially teachings on sexuality. Research has shown that the great majority of married Catholics make up their own minds about sexuality in family life. There is another contrary strand of thinking which proposes that the encyclical was a timely counter-cultural and prophetic statement against the perceived hedonism of self-indulgent sexuality.

As new insights in the social sciences, cosmology, anthropology and theology emerge, church teachings, in the words of a religious psychologist Ken Wilber, should 'transcend and include' and 'negate and preserve' the process of reformulating doctrines. In other words, we honour past experiences and beliefs in the Christian tradition. However, our own contemporary life experiences and new knowledge enable us to either incorporate new wisdoms into previous beliefs or let go of past beliefs or teachings that reflect a mindset of past times. Slavery was not condemned by the church until 1882. To act otherwise is to fossilise church teachings. The Christian community, like the whole universe, is on an unfolding evolutionary journey. The Good News is too precious and relevant to be relegated to a religious museum.

Conclusion

A reflection on the Genesis origin myth generates many questions about how the literalism of interpretation raised problems of reconciling its interpretation with the findings of evolutionary science. Research on the evolution of the human species is challenging Christians to reshape their understanding of the human person and reorientate their Christology.

There was no point in time or space where a singular morally bad act occurred in our evolutionary past. There was no one-off moment of defiance of a God who condemned all humanity into a sinful heritage.

The following chapter explores how the Genesis origin myth may be interpreted as an Emergence not as Fall.

CHAPTER FIVE

The story of emergence

In this chapter, the Genesis origin myth is interpreted as Emergence not as Fall. The act of taking fruit from the Tree of Knowledge is portrayed as a crucial symbol of humankind crossing an evolutionary threshold into self-reflective consciousness as the emergence of *homo sapiens*. Humankind now begins the great archetypal journey of enlightenment. Historically, there have been, and are now, several explanations for the life, death and mission of Jesus who became the Christ. If the Genesis origin myth is interpreted as Emergence not Fall, then there needs to be a new emphasis on the mission of Jesus. The traditionally dominant Atonement explanation of the mission of Jesus no longer has credence in contemporary consciousness.

The tree of knowledge symbol

Is the Fall from grace the only interpretation of the sacred myth of Genesis or is there an alternative interpretation of the story as the beginning of the great journey of humankind? If the story is interpreted as a symbolic story about the beginning of the journey of consciousness, then the Christ story is more about the ongoing flowering of our humanity in Christ than picking up the pieces of a divine plan that went wrong.

By choosing to eat the fruit of the Tree of Knowledge knowing good and evil, humans plunged into the vagaries of life with all its joys and sorrows. The need to work, *by the sweat of your face you shall eat bread* (Genesis 3:19) is a directive about being co-creators rather than receiving a punishment for disobedience. It is proposed that the action of Adam and Eve in taking the fruit of the Tree of Knowledge may be understood as the symbol for the emergence of self-consciousness humans. That symbolic action is described by palaeontologists when they speculate on how and when the hominids or early humans crossed a threshold into self-consciousness and emerged as *homo sapiens*.

In eating the fruit from the Tree of Knowledge, humans inherit the power to make moral choices. They do good deeds and they sin. They can choose between God's providential care and their own freedom. They have to work for their livelihood, struggle against the whims of nature and experience pain in childbirth (Genesis 3:16-19). By taking the fruit of the Tree of Knowledge, humans inherit an evolutionary impulse for creative energy and intelligence to innovate and express their deepest desires. Humans are now fully involved in the evolutionary development of creation. For a person of faith, God and humans together are active participants within the whole process of creation with all its whims and vagaries, twists and turns in the evolutionary journey of **becoming**. The **becoming** is a movement from the static consciousness of the paradise garden to an act of self-consciousness and ultimately to a unity with God. There is a purpose in the evolutionary ongoing story of creation.

Human hubris

The myth sends out a stern message about the misuse of knowledge through eating the forbidden fruit from the Tree of Knowledge. Hubris is a regular refrain in the human story. In Greek mythology, Icarus, ignoring the advice of his father, flies too close to the sun with his wax wings and plunges into the sea when the sun melts the wax. An ever present temptation for humans is to assume the role of arrogant 'gods' in ways that utilise scientific knowledge to pillage the earth. Humans develop nuclear weapons and sometimes use science without ethics. Their hubris knows no bounds in making decisions without regard for what is good or evil, *your eyes will be opened and you will be like God, knowing good and evil* (Genesis 3:4). The third temptation experienced by Jesus in the desert is a replica of the first temptation to Eve. Satan tempts Jesus, *All these things I will give you, if you fall down and worship me* (Matthew 4: 9). Jesus answers Satan by saying that humans must recognise both the glories and the limits of their own humanity as created by the living God. Humans are not to assume god-like powers to determine the fate of others.

The explosions of atomic bombs on Nagasaki and Hiroshima in August 1945 were terrifying symbols of humanity's propensity to play 'god'. The dawn of the 20th century seemed to inaugurate a new era of optimism through inventions of electricity, cars, aeroplanes, wireless and other technologies. The hubris of humanity knew no bounds. However, on 15 April 1912, nature, in the form of a giant iceberg, tore the heart out of the greatest passenger ship ever built, the *Titanic*. The doomed ship plunged to the sea bottom in just over two hours. Two years later, in 1914, the world was plunged in the horrors of World War I leaving behind its heritage of ten million dead. The unbridled utilisation of modern technology to advance the skill of mechanised slaughter of world wars in the 20th century heralded a new era of human hubris and sin. Demonic science gassed millions of Jews in the concentration camps. The headlong rush into nuclear energy without weighing up the problems of what to do with nuclear waste and protection against natural disasters to nuclear stations has generated unresolved social and environmental issues (c.f. McDonagh).

Journey of enlightenment

The loss of the living in the paradise garden was the first step in the transformation of human consciousness. The dream of harmony dissolved into the reality of life. The expulsion from the Eden garden became the catalyst for beginning the journey of enlightenment. Scientists report how the size and capacity of human brains evolved over thousands of years. As our brains developed, consciousness emerged into new levels of awareness about human destiny and ecological connectedness. Humans had to deal with the ultimate destiny of death. Self-conscious beings learned to adjust to the whims of nature. Through trial and error humans, discovered ways to cope with climate changes.

The myth of the Paradise garden is a symbol pointing to an inner dream for the attainment of harmony in creation. There is something deep within the human psyche which urges us towards such harmony. We long for peace and reconciliation. We hope that all people have food and security. We wish that all people, regardless of ethnic type, religious belief or national identity learn to live together cooperatively. The 'yin/yan' mandala expresses symbolically the oneness of all things, darkness and light existing together as one. In his teaching, Jesus expounded on the Paradise theme which he called the 'Kingdom of God', a dream for wholeness or 'abundance of life' (John 10:10).

The Genesis myth symbolically describes the reality of living in a complex evolving world. In the myth, humankind has now taken the first steps to leave forever the primal state of a closed Eden consciousness. Humans are expelled from the garden and there is no going back, *He drove out the man; and at the east of the garden of Eden he placed the cherubim, and a sword flaming and turning to guard the way to the tree of life* (Genesis 3:24). Once the evolutionary journey has begun there is no return to a state of static consciousness. Humanity cannot go back to a social patriarchal structures, slavery, autocracy, tribal consciousness or ecological vandalism. Humanity must move forward to a sustainable global way of being. The prospect of regression to the destruction of a life support system for the whole web of life in creation is unthinkable.

In their evolutionary history, human beings emerge from closed consciousness to a capability for self-reflection and freedom to make moral choices. They can now experience the past as well as the present and have also imbibed a fear of death. The origin myth describes how humans became aware of their separateness from each other and their separateness from nature, *Then their eyes were opened, and they knew that they were naked; and they sewed fig leaves together and they made loincloths for themselves* (Genesis 3:7). The development of symbolic consciousness empowered humans to reflect on their life situations and relationships with the earth and the world of spirits. The religious historian Karen Armstrong wrote that her study of religion led her to conclude, *that human beings are spiritual animals. Indeed there is a case for arguing that Homo sapiens is also Homo religious* (1999:3).

The archetypal journey is becoming more 'awake', more aware to self, others and nature. Buddha means, 'I am awake'. The awakening in consciousness is becoming more receptive to what is happening around us through listening and observing. Jesus enjoined his followers to *Keep awake* (Mark 14:38). A general consciousness, rather than a closed introspective vision, enables a person to be more aware of people's life situations. Becoming more aware of others is the pathway to compassion. Being aware or 'awake' links us with a transpersonal consciousness of universal empathy and love.

The English biologist Rupert Sheldrake proposed an interesting theory that suggested systems are surrounded by non-visible energy fields that carry information from one generation to the next. His hypothesis of 'morphic resonance' considered how the human person is a field of energy and this field of energy can extend across to others (Cannato: 7). From my studies of shamanistic experiences, the power of prayer, the doctrine of communion of saints and after-death visions to loved ones (c.f. Nowotny-Keane), I believe the theory of 'morphic resonance' has some validity. Positive energy and compassion towards others can, and does, influence others for good.

The nature of a human person is not exclusively egoistical to look after self at the expense of others. Altruism, that is human behaviour directed towards the wellbeing of others, is an essential element to being human. The selfish gene theory of Neo-Darwinism (survival of the fittest) has been questioned. Empathy, love and compassion are as integral to the human nature as is self-centredness. People are born and live in a world of original grace. People are also born and live in a world of turmoil, natural disasters, ethical struggles, hungers and oppression, living and dying within the cycle of creation. People love and hate. They make peace and war. Sin, both personal and structural, exists side by side with love and compassion.

As civilisations became more complex in social organisations, humans gradually established moral codes which governed the social lives of their communities. These moral codes evolved around matters relating to families, community relations, the common good and relationships between the sexes. Religions provided a moral glue to hold these ethical codes together. A universal ethic which encompassed all codes is stated as, *Do unto others as you wish people would do unto you* or *love your neighbour as yourself.* The

Golden Rule for living compassionately is held by all religious traditions e.g. *This is the sum of duty: do not do to others what would cause pain if done to you* (Hinduism); *Not one of you truly believes, until you wish for others what you wish for yourself* (Islam); *In everything, do to others as you would have them do to you* (Christianity). Any code of ethics has to take into account an evolutionary understanding of human beings. For example, only recently has a growing ecological consciousness jolted Christians into the moral imperatives of stewardship, earth sustainability and animal rights. Indigenous peoples have lived these moral imperatives for thousands of years and have much earth wisdoms to share.

The archetypal journey

The great journey of life is an enduring motif in all cultures. Many origin myths describe the archetypal journey. There is an inner restlessness in the human species which urges them ever onwards to explore new lands and seek new frontiers of knowledge. It is deep within human nature to be driven beyond our own limitations. According to Cohen, we are always seeking higher truths. He writes, '*Why do we at times feel compelled to improve ourselves, not only for our own sake, but for the sake of a higher cause that we can sense yet barely see?* (3).

The first humans emerged out of Africa and spread across the globe. The emergence impulse within humans involves taking risks and being pathfinders. Early humans discovered fire and ways of protection against marauding predators. Twelve thousand years ago humans discovered a grass called wheat which became the sustenance for farming communities. In 1492, Columbus kept sailing west until he discovered the islands of the Bahamas. Scientists continue researching to discover innovative forms of transport and new medicines. Explorers keep climbing formidable mountain peaks. The latest iPad becomes yesterday's product within months as cyber technicians accelerate the speed of the technical discovery journey. We are always in a process of *becoming*.

The archetypal journey is a journey of enlightenment. Many cultures have journey stories about the quest for the Holy Grail. Gautama, the Buddha, leaves his family and begins his journey to find the meaning of suffering. The Greek hero Odysseus travels on his journey homewards after the fall of Troy. In the *Gilgamesh Epic*, Gilgamesh goes in search of immortality after the death of his friend. Abram was commanded by the Lord, *Go from your country... to the land that I will show you* (Genesis 12:1). The Jewish people flee from the wrath of the Egyptians and wander for forty years in the desert in the exodus journey towards the Promised Land. In the gospel of Luke, two disillusioned disciples encounter the Stranger on the journey from Jerusalem to Emmaus (Luke 24). The Acts of the Apostles is an account of the evangelising journey of early Christians. Mohammed travels to Mecca in 630. The Pilgrim Fathers (and mothers) sail from England in 1620 for the Promised Land in the New World. The theme of 'homecoming' is a refrain in diverse archetypal journeys. The theme of 'homecoming' is especially highlighted in indigenous spiritualities as a journey to communion with the earth and the Creator Spirit(s) (c.f. Hall & Hendriks).

The archetypal journey is both an external journey of moving from a state of security and an internal journey towards enlightenment. According to Carl Jung, the interior journey of individuation is integrating the conscious and unconscious to allow the *Imago Dei* to infuse one whole being. Jung's comment on the life journey is perceptive, 'Do you want to go through life walking upright or dragged through by a series of events'. In other words, do you want to seek insight on what is happening or else be mindlessly buffeted by the ebb and flow of life events?

Life journey commentators suggest that the first phase of a person's life is concerned with such ego needs as security, status, attending to institutional imperatives and setting boundaries. The second half of life is moving to the world within and engaging the interior deep concerns of the soul. The interior journey is a journey for wisdom. Jung described the first part of life as composing the script. The second part of life is a commentary on the script. Medieval theologians believed that the *questio* (Latin for 'seek') always preceded the idea. It is in the nature of humans to be wanderers, explorers and discoverers. If the journey to the moon on 21 July 1969 is not far enough, then space travel has now set its sights on a journey to Mars. The landing of the space vehicle *Curiosity* on Mars on 6 August 2012 will continue to open up new vistas on the universe. Mars is now the new space frontier.

Pilgrimages are a common facet of all religions. The word 'pilgrim' comes from the Latin word 'peregrinus' meaning 'to wander about'. The pilgrimage for the Muslim faithful to Mecca is the Fifth Pillar of Islam. In the Middle Ages, the four major pilgrimages for Christians were to Jerusalem, Rome, Canterbury and Compostela in Santiago. In more recent times, participation in Christian pilgrimages has been revived. The Camino de Santiago de Compostela or 'Way of St James' pilgrimage is now experiencing a new wave of popularity. Stories about pilgrimages highlight the mixed motives for pilgrims in going on pilgrimages. An underlying theme for many pilgrims seems to be a desire for spiritual growth and enlightenment.

Before we propose how the Jesus story may be told within an evolutionary perspective, it is helpful to reflect on how traditional interpretations of the Genesis origin myth have shaped the Christian story.

Christian interpretations of the Genesis origin myth

St Paul was probably the only theologian who did not have access to written gospels. His letters were written in the 40s and 50s, perhaps twenty years before the first gospel of Mark. However, he would have known those who knew Jesus personally. As a pious and learned Jew, he situated the Christ story within the Jewish framework of the Fall. In the Epistle to the Romans, Paul explains the meaning of Christ's suffering and death within the context of the Fall tradition. He interprets the Fall myth literally, *Therefore just as one man's trespass led to condemnation for all, so one man's act of righteousness leads to justification and life for all. For just as by one man's disobedience the many were made sinners, so by one man's obedience, the many will be made righteousness* (Romans 5:18).

At this point in the text, I alert the reader to a complex theological issue which is relevant to the topic but well beyond the scope of this book to expound. The issue concerns the relationship of the writings of Paul to the Jesus story as told by the four gospels. Because Paul's interpretation of the mission of Jesus as Christ has shaped the character of Christology, are there other perspectives on how the mission of Jesus might be understood?

The topic of filters in uncovering the real historical Jesus has stimulated spirited theological debate throughout centuries. Is the character of Christianity which we have inherited a true reflection of the historical Jesus, or is it rather a product of the 'Paulinism' of the Epistles? The philosopher Martin Buber once wrote, 'The Jesus of the Sermon on the Mount is completely opposed to Paul'. Perhaps we will never know the answer to that question. Recent biblical scholarship has reservations about any overemphasis on the distinctions between Christ of the gospels and the Christ of the epistles (c.f. Elmer).

A further issue is trying to discover the historical Jesus from the portraits of Jesus in the four Christian communities represented by the gospels of Mark, Matthew, Mark, and John. Jesus as a Jew spoke and preached in Aramaic and could read Hebrew. The problem of filters is compounded by the fact that the gospels were written in Greek which is vastly different from Aramaic in its modes of thought. Aramaic is a very poetic form of language with many possible interpretations to words. The gospel authors, writing in Greek, had to make specific choices of words in translating the preaching of Jesus in Aramaic.

Historical interpretation of the mission of Jesus

If we consider the various interpretations of the meaning of the death of Jesus, we note that there have been several explanations for the mission of Jesus throughout the course of Christian history. For the disciples, the sudden and violent death of Jesus was a shocking experience. They sought explanations for this tragedy.

The gospels were composed by authors steeped in the religious assumptions of Judaism. The gospels of Matthew, Mark and Luke were written by people living within the religious writings and synagogue rituals of Judaism. The account of the crucifixion and death of Jesus was clearly influenced by the very important Jewish feast of Yom Kippur (literally: 'day of atonement') where a bull was slaughtered for the sins of the people (Leviticus 16:11). The Suffering Servant in the writings of Isaiah (Ch 53) was a prototype of the Suffering Servant of Jesus. The story of Abraham's obedience to God's command to sacrifice his son (Genesis 22) provided a framework for Christian worship (see Letter to the Hebrews). For New Testament writers steeped in Temple worship which involved the sacrifice of animals as an expiation for sin, one obvious explanation for his shedding of blood on the cross was a supreme sacrificial act of reparation to God for the sins of humankind (see 1 Peter 1:18-19).

Another explanation for the death of Jesus was the idea of the metaphor of 'ransom'. In New Testament times (and one might add in modern times when ransoms are paid to Somalia pirates), a ransom was paid to set free captured eminent people (see Mark 10:45). Through the death of his Son, God was paying a ransom to Satan to set people free from their sin. Theologians such as Origen, Ambrose, Augustine and John Chrysostom supported this explanation.

A third explanation, which became a dominant one in Christian theology to present times, was the Atonement theory. This theory had its origins in New Testament writings. In the Letter to the Hebrews, we read, *Therefore he (Jesus) had to become like his brothers and sisters in every respect, so that he might be a merciful and faithful high priest in the service of God, to make a sacrifice of atonement for the sins of the* people (2:17). This view was expanded by St Anselm of Canterbury (1033-1109) and quickly gained currency in theological circles. Anselm held that because of the first sin, the cosmic order had been distorted and needed to be set right again. In the medieval cultural environment, if a person abused or dishonoured the authority of his lord, he was required to make reparation or satisfaction to the lord. Applying this theory to the story of Adam and Eve, it was held that Adam and Eve had offended God as an infinite Being. Hence only Jesus as God and human was worthy to make satisfaction on our behalf (Romans 5:6-7).

In our contemporary consciousness, the very idea that a loving God would require the horrible death of his Son on Calvary is quite repulsive. The Atonement theory was affirmed at the Council of Trent (1545-1563) and continues to hold official status in church teaching. The *Catechism of the Catholic Church* states, *Jesus atoned for our sins and made satisfaction for our sins to the Father* (n 615; c.f. Council of Trent 1547 DS 1529).

Historically there have been other explanations for the death of Jesus.

St Irenaeus of Lyons (d c 200), one of the most influential theologians in early Christianity, proposed that Jesus as God's perfect creation was integral to the whole evolutionary process of creation. Creation was not a one-off event. God was continually creating, evolving and perfecting creation. According to St Irenaeus, redemption was a positive act of healing in the perfecting of creation. Rather than rectifying a plan that went wrong, the redemptive mission of Jesus as the Christ was to bring humanity to wholeness within creation.

The Moral Influence theory, first taught by Peter Abelard (1079-1147), held that the painful death that Jesus endured showed how much God loves us and should move us to respond in gratitude and repentance for such an extraordinary self-sacrifice (Smith 1996:200-204). In Protestant theology (especially John Calvin), the suffering on Calvary becomes a 'substitute' for humanity. Jesus puts himself in our place as a 'substitute' instead of us. It is Jesus who suffers for the sins of humanity. Protestant redemption theology tended to emphasise human depravity more than the Catholic and Orthodox tradition.

While we appreciate the cultural context of each of these explanations for the death of Jesus, none of these explanations make much sense to contemporary cultural consciousness if taken literally. These explanations are also at odds with established findings on biological evolution. In the 2000 years of Christianity, there are many layers of explanations of how Christ is understood in his mission. He has been, and is regarded now as, Redeemer, Saviour, Light of the World, Healer, Liberator, 'First Born of Creation' (Colossians 1:15) and many other titles. Each of these titles is appropriate for an evolutionary appreciation of the mission of Jesus.

The Franciscan tradition of Christology was more positive about our humanity and Christ in creation and complemented the dominant Fall/redemption tradition in Christology. In more recent times, feminist and liberation theologies teach a Christ through the lens of gender equity and freedom from oppression. The Orthodox tradition was more attuned to a positive view of the Incarnation than the Fall-Redemption theme in Western Christianity.

Sacrificial language

Sacrificial language still permeates Christian worship such as, 'sacrifice of the Mass'. The concept of 'sacrifice' language in liturgy does not sit easily in contemporary consciousness. What does today's person make of this description of the Eucharist in the *Catechism of the Catholic Church: The Holy Sacrifice, because it makes present the one sacrifice of Christ the Saviour and includes the Church's offering. The terms 'holy sacrifice of the Mass', 'sacrifice of praise', 'spiritual sacrifice', 'pure and holy sacrifice' are also used, since it completes and surpasses all the sacrifices of the Old Covenant* (n 1330)? What a contrast to the simplicity of the Last Supper!

There would be no problem with using the word 'sacrifice' if its use was related to its meaning from Latin. In Latin, *sacrificium* means 'to make holy'. The movement towards union with God implies a letting go of what inhibits this union. The self-emptying of 'kenosis' describes the utter commitment of Jesus as Christ, *who though he was in the form of God, did not regard equality with God as something to be exploited, but emptied himself taking the form of a slave* (Philippians 2:7). Describing the Eucharist meal as the 'sacrifice of the Mass' tends to evoke an image of a priest offering up a Victim Christ as an act of appeasement to God. The concept of the Mass as 'a sacrifice' places undue emphasis on the active role of the priest as **the** one offering the sacrifice while the laity in the congregation are passive observers to the sacrificial action of the priest. Sacrificial language for priesthood suggests priesthood as a cultic ministry rather than a servant presider of the Christian community at Eucharist worship.

A dilemma for Christians today is reconciling the dominant sacrificial language of the New Testament as an explanation for the death of Jesus on Calvary with an interpretation of the Genesis origin myth as Emergence not Fall. Out of respect for a venerable tradition of liturgical prayer, there are no easy answers to this dilemma. Perhaps a gradual raising awareness about the issue of sacrificial language and allowing language in worship and theology to find its own level at the appropriate time will settle as a compromise. Because the sacrifice language is here to stay in liturgy, maybe it is best to highlight the 'make holy' meaning of 'sacrifice' and leave it there.

The reality of sin

If we view the Genesis origin myth as Emergence not Fall, there is certainly no suggestion of denying the harsh reality of sin, both personal and structural sin. I was startled when someone who heard about the title of my book asked me, 'Are you really suggesting doing away with sin? What planet do you live on?'

Once we begin to talk about things relating to God, then we are challenged to consider the mystery of evil. The anguished cry 'Why?' 'Why?' echoes in every generation about terrible things that happen. Everyday our media reports a plethora of events which only too well illustrate the human propensity to sin. Domestic violence, wars, suicide bombings, famine, murder, rape, greed, financial misdeeds, ecological vandalism - the list goes on as a depressing commentary about human inclination to commit sin. A reflection on the horrors of the Shoah (Holocaust), The Gulags of the Stalin era, the regime of Pol Pot and Rwanda massacres can leave one almost despairing about the goodness of the human race.

A few years ago, I visited the small town of Oradour-sur-Glane near Limoges, France. As I wandered through the desecrated town, I pondered on the horror of what happened on 10 June 1944 when SS Panzer Division Das Reich wrought their barbaric vengeance on a hapless people. The sober reality of human sinfulness was starkly portrayed in the eerily silent streets and the burnt out church where many of the villagers were locked in the church and incinerated. The scratch marks on the church walls made by people being burned alive in the church remain as symbols of pure evil.

We don't need to hold a belief that sin entered the world through a primal act of disobedience. There has never been a time where humans have not failed morally. When human beings evolved into the ability of self-consciousness, they also inherited the power of make moral choices for good or evil. St Paul vividly describes the inner struggle between good and evil within each person, *I do not understand my own actions. For I do not do what I want, but I do the very thing I hate... but sin dwells within me* (Romans 7:15-16).It is in their very nature for every person to possess a Tree of Knowledge within their own human identity, to choose good or evil. Evil is 'live' spelt backwards. Neuroscience has demonstrated that we are wired for both inclinations towards good and bad, cooperation and selfishness. Our own need for self protection can lead us to hurting others. Sin is something against the gift of life. To be free we must always have the option and freedom of choosing something that is not good. The etymology of the word 'sin' is related to archery. An arrow fired at the target misses the target (Greek: *hamartia*: 'missing the mark'). Sin is 'missing the target' of being a fully human person.

Our very sinfulness offers a moral vulnerability to the prospect of grace. The Dominican Meister Eckhart (c1260-1327) wrote, 'I can give you no better advice than to find God where you lost him'. The younger son in the parable of the Two Sons and the Merciful Father (Luke 15:11-32) experiences the graced forgiveness of his father only after he recognised and acknowledged his absolute destitution and belief in his father's forgiveness. The brokenness of sin throws us down into the depths of our human vulnerability. It is in these very depths that grace awaits those who choose to be enfolded by God's loving embrace. The cross of the crucified Jesus is a sign of hope not of despair.

The Genesis origin myth interpreted as Emergence and not as Fall proposes in symbolic language that sin did not enter the nature of the human species because of purported act of disobedience by Adam and Eve. Making moral choices is integral to the evolution of humans as they evolved into a state of self-reflective consciousness. Human beings have the freedom to choose good or evil. The Genesis origin myth may be understood as a symbolic process of moving to a higher plane of consciousness while having to pay the price of the suffering involved in an evolutionary leap forwards. A new order of creation comes at a cost. Everything in creation dies or becomes extinct. The Fall is not a downwards movement but an evolutionary 'fall upward' (Edwards 1999:61). Adam and Eve, as a symbol of the human race, could never be fully human people unless they were capable of making moral choices.

Conclusion

This chapter has looked at the interpretation of the Genesis Origin myth as a mythical story about the Emergence of human consciousness and not as a Fall from grace. An interpretation of the origin myth describes the beginning of the long journey of humankind with all the ebbs and flows of human destiny, including making moral choices for good or evil. The chapter also highlights the inadequacy of the Fall tradition if the myth is interpreted literally as a framework to develop a Christology which accords with contemporary consciousness. The mission of Jesus who became the Christ was not a divine rescue mission, but a revelation of God's limitless love within an expanded religious consciousness in an evolving universe.

The following chapters consider what this interpretation as Emergence means for practical Christianity.

CHAPTER SIX

Recognising the 'signs of the times' in an emergence vision

The Jesus story is always told within the context of a cultural environment. This chapter considers some significant cultural movements which influence the character of the Christian story. The term, 'signs of the times' became a popular rallying cry from the Second Vatican Council. What are some of the 'signs of the times' in today's world?

The need to be attuned to the cultural environment for effective evangelisation

What are the implications for Christian living if we situate the Christ story within a framework of Emergence rather than Fall? Where are the points of continuity and discontinuity with traditional Christian theology and worship?

Much of the Christian story is unchanged within an Emergence perspective. The Nicene Creed continues as a basic creedal statement although its archaic language needs a more contemporary expression (Treston: 157-158; MacGregor 189-211). The mission of Christ assumes enriched understandings to explain the sufferings, death and resurrection of Jesus as Christ. Some liturgical prayers are modified to replace the notion of humanity recovering from the consequences of the Fall.

The task of reconciling and incorporating the Fall tradition with its venerable heritage of devotions, spirituality, liturgy and theology into a Christian vision which is more attuned to an Emergence perspective awaits future generations of scholars. The next *Summa* should not be written solely by theologians. The next *Summa* will be the fruits of a composition by a creative partnership between theologians, scientists, cosmologists, historians (including inter-faith historians), spiritual guides, poets and social scientists with an underlying grounding by the lived experience of ordinary faithful Christians.

This chapter focuses on naming some features of the cultural landscape for telling the Christ story as a story of Emergence. An evolutionary lens for telling the Christian story highlights how external events shape the consciousness of the interior life and structures of the church. After considering a selection of cultural movements that impact of the Christ story, the following chapter will delve into the Jesus story itself.

'Signs of the times'

A foundational theme in exploring the Christian story from an evolutionary perspective is reflecting on the 'signs of the times' or being more aware of the cultural context for the gospel (inculturation). At the time of the Second Vatican Council (1962-1965), the phrase 'signs of the times' became an imperative for Christian involvement in the dynamics of the world. The Vatican II Document, *Pastoral Constitution on the Church in the Modern World* urges Christians to be attentive to what was happening in the world so as to transform society. Such a transformation would better reflect the justice and harmony of God's kingdom. If Christians are locked into the 'Two World' dichotomy of Augustine, viewing religion as separate from world, a City of God and a City of World, then they see no need to take seriously the challenge of reading the 'signs of the times'.

'Two World' people view religion and society as existing on parallel lines but rarely interacting with one another. My own experience as a consultant in diocesan pastoral planning over the years taught me sober lessons about the studied indifference from some church leaders when they were presented with research from parish and diocesan surveys. The research was dismissed as, 'So what?' and considered as irrelevant to parish and diocesan planning. To 'read the signs of the times' is not performing a mindless kowtow to the latest cultural buzz. On the contrary, reading the 'signs of the times' is a discerned awareness of what is happening in society which impacts on the proclamation of the gospel. If Christians take the incarnation (John 1:14) seriously, then those communicating the gospel will be attentive to the heartbeats of their cultural environment.

An evolutionary perspective on the Christ story

A basic concern for any consideration of the implications of Emergence not Fall for the Christ story is an acceptance of the reality of the evolution of all things in creation, including the evolution of the human species. An evolutionary world view has far reaching implications for how we understand the human story, culture, cosmology, science and envision the future.

There are two contrasting attitudes to evolution in church life.

An attitude of **classical consciousness** holds the timelessness of religious truths, church doctrines and structures. An alternative view is **historical consciousness** which is comfortable with how language, world views and cultural symbols evolve over the years. In the lens of historical consciousness, the Genesis origin myth may be interpreted as a symbolic expression of the evolutionary nature of all things in creation, including the evolution of the human species. Attitudes to ethnic groups, pluralism of religions, sexual identity, ecological concerns, justice and the status of women are examples of how social attitudes evolve in higher levels of consciousness. Pope Pius IX could say on 29 June 1866, 'It is not contrary to the natural and divine law for a slave to be sold, bought, exchanged or given'.

In future years, we can be sure of people in 2070 saying about people in 2013, 'How could they ever think things like that?' Anyone who has reservations about the evolution of doctrine in church teachings should spend time reading church history. For example, compare Pope Boniface VIII's proclamation *(Unam Sanctam)* in 1302, *Extra ecclesiam, nulla salus* ('outside the church there is no salvation') with the document *Declaration on Religious Freedom* (1965) in the Second Vatican Council. This document overturned at least 1,500 years of church teaching. In 1324, Pope John XXII condemned the doctrine of infallibility as the work of the devil, the father of all lies. The First Vatican Council (1870) proclaimed that the doctrine of papal infallibility was to be held by all Catholics.

To live Christianity within an Emergence perspective is to accept that beliefs are articulated in different ways than were expressed in previous generations. The pre-scientific assumptions of the biblical world no longer are intelligible in a scientific environment. A modern person cannot imagine how a person could walk on water or raise a person from the dead. However, the inner message of the Bible is even more relevant today.

An example of how language changes is the example of the use of the word 'transubstantiation' to describe the mystery of the transformed bread and wine into Christ's Body and Blood. In the Middle Ages, theologians drew their language from the Greek philosopher Aristotle to describe the mystery of bread and wine becoming the Body and Blood of Christ. They used the term 'transubstantiation': the substance changes into the Body and Blood of Christ but the form does not. Such a philosophical term is meaningless today unless we modify the meaning to suggest a symbolic 'transubstantiation' or inner transformation which happens within each person who participates in the Eucharistic celebration.

We have already discussed the various theologies formulated throughout the ages to explain the death and resurrection as Atonement. Today the very idea of a vengeful Deity demanding a horrific death of his Son is unthinkable. Blessed John Henry Newman's (d1890) essay on the development of doctrine described how doctrines are expressed differently over the ages through the lived faith of the community. The lived experience of the faithful acts as a catalyst for changes to occur in the formulation and practices of beliefs. The role of the *sensus fidelium* (lived experience of the faithful) is an essential element in evangelisation. When Church leadership becomes remote from the *sensus fidelium*, Church teachings have little impact on the lives of the faithful because the teachings no longer reflect the lived reality of the gospel. Unless the laity (including Religious) are fully involved in the process of the 'new evangelisation' movement, it will bear little fruit. The ancient saying 'people support what they create' is as relevant to church life as it is to business leadership.

If the Incarnation means anything, the Christian story will always be firmly embedded in the ebb and flow of world events and consciousness. Evangelisation, or sharing the Good News, is not experienced in a vacuum but encountering people in specific times and places within the historical evolution of the world. Grace awaits our lived realities. Although our culture is suspicious of any grand overarching cultural narratives such as the narrative of Christianity, I believe that the Christian story has much to offer contemporary civilisation. In an era of cultural diversity and religious pluralism, the reign of any religion offering a meta-narrative is long gone, at least in countries with a traditional Christian ethos. Christianity can choose to hide away as a remnant religious relic under siege or it can plunge into the swirling waters of evolutionary change, trusting in the Spirit and discerning leadership.

What are key 'signs of the times' in our world and how might these 'signs' impact on an evolutionary understanding of the Christian story?

Selected themes in a cultural landscape

The following comments are not intended as a summary of social trends in Western orientated countries. The topics chosen are not necessarily relevant to cultures not shaped by Western values. Rather the topics are offered as a series of random brush strokes across the cultural landscape of Western orientated countries.

A world in transition

One hardly needs to produce any evidence to verify that the world is now culturally in rapid transition. Change is all around us and the speed of change is bewildering. For example, the speed of change in the incremental use of cyber technology can quickly leave people adrift of the latest innovation. It is almost incomprehensible to realise the widespread use of internet is only a few decades old. A young generation cannot envisage a world without iPhones, iPads, mobile phones, Facebook, Twitter and so on.

Social networking in cyber space has opened up new ways of relating, connecting and collaborating. The most mundane event in one's life, such as having a cup of coffee is shared on Facebook or Twitter. Thousands of people are marshalled for justice causes through internet appeals. On an average, I receive daily five appeals via internet or Facebook to support justice or environmental causes. I will say nothing about the proliferation of scams which amaze me to learn every so often that I have won untold millions of dollars in lotteries in which I have never even bought a ticket!

During the 1970s, Marshall McLuhan's concept of a global village seemed a radical idea. Now such a concept is assumed as a given. Old certainties have disappeared. Cultural norms seem to be in an ever evolving metamorphosis into a global monoculture although not necessarily for people of Islamic faith. Such rapid cultural transitions leave some people disorientated. People may ask, 'Where are communal certainties?' 'What is left of my religious faith to believe in?'

Religious and political fundamentalism thrive in a climate of radical change. The rise of religious and political fundamentalism is based on fear. Questions and statements such as the following reflect cultural and religious anxiety about change: 'What will happen to my belief system if you tell me that some of my beliefs need to be understood in a different way?' 'How will I cope with all this change?' 'I'm really angry with those people who threaten the world I believed in with all these new ideas'. (c.f. Armstrong 2000: Introduction).

An expanding and evolving universe

Our origins stretch back to the creation of the stars and ultimately to the primeval fireball of the Big Bang. We are the first generation to possess some scientific knowledge about the origins of the universe. For thousands of years, people assumed that the earth was the centre of the cosmos. Copernicus (1473-1543) proposed that the sun, not the earth, was the centre of our galaxy. Galileo's telescope (1619) uncovered a sky with millions of stars. Hubble's space telescope, launched in 1990, circles the earth transmitting astonishing images of cosmic space enabling scientists to explore the almost limitless expanse of the universe. The space vehicle *Curiosity*, launched in 2012, transmits breathtaking photos of the planet Mars. Modern cosmology reveals an immense universe of billions of galaxies with billions of stars, supernovas (explosions of dying stars), black holes, dark matter and even speculations about a multi-verse, that is, the existence of many universes.

It would seem that humanity's relationship with the earth changed forever when astronauts, circling the earth in July 1969, beamed back to the earth that famous picture. The earth was shown as a tiny blue blob floating in an eerie space without horizons. A three tiered biblical world view has long been discarded and the message of the Bible has to be interpreted and communicated within the context of modern cosmology.

Darwin in his *Origin of Species* (1859) demonstrated the evolutionary nature of species through natural selection. All evolution is co-evolution because individual evolutions of species affect other species. In more recent times, quantum physics has explained how everything in creation is interrelated and in a state of flux and change. Evolutionary science has shown how the human species has evolved over millions of years. Threats to ecological wellbeing are slowly calling people back to issues of eco-justice and earth care.

Globalisation, economics and science

Modern communications have rapidly augmented the process of globalisation. In one sense, global communications have virtually abolished space and distance. News of a war, a terrorist bombing or tsunami is disseminated instantly throughout the cyber world. William Calvin suggests that our brains are changing and being rewired as 'intelligence augmentation' to cope with the new ways of knowing through the internet. Meeting friends has a new dimension with the internet. A Blondie cartoon captures the difference between generations. In the cartoon, Dagwood tells his daughter he would like to meet her friends. The daughter is really happy about that request. She brings Dagwood to her computer and opens Facebook saying, 'Here are my friends, Daddy!'

Money has become a global enterprise. A financial crisis in one major country can trigger panic on the global stock market. National governments are often relatively helpless to cushion the impact of global recession. Constant media updates on the latest Euro crisis and the USA debt crisis send shivers through stock markets and generate communal insecurity.

Huge industrial companies, whose budget exceeds the budgets of many countries, are not bound by national borders and flourish as self-contained transnational enterprises. These mega-companies control enormous finances and resources of the planet. Their core value is to maximise profits. They bring riches and employment to economies but their self-contained entities can also pillage the planet with impunity. The new social order of this century is not held together by a monarchy or aristocratic class as previously in history but now by global economic companies. An oft repeated question by social commentators about some proposal for development is, 'Will it be good for the economy?' rather than, 'How are people and the planetary health affected by this proposal?'

Capitalism is the modus operandi for most developed countries of the world. Inherent in the ideology of capitalism is competition rather than communal cooperation. Extreme capitalism reduces people to instruments of work for the generation of wealth that is concentrated into the hands of a chosen few. Pope Benedict (2005- 2013) in his encyclical *Caritas in Veritate* (Charity in Truth) expressed his deep concern about the growing gap between rich and poor and how consumerism focused on 'having more' rather than 'being more'. Natural resources are treated as expendable resources for the accumulation of wealth. Planetary health suffers from this irresponsible exploitation. The theme of common good struggles to be heard amidst a cacophony of siren calls for profits and excessive wealth. There is nothing wrong with wealth creation provided it is also concerned with social justice that leads to a more participative society. With USA and Europe in a debt spiral, it would seem that there can be no real world economic recovery without the restoration of civic virtue and a commitment to an ethos of social responsibility.

During the last century, there has developed a formidable corpus of church teachings about wealth distribution, worker's rights and the common good. However, the power of mass consumerism is so woven into the very fabric of people's lives and consciousness that it will take prophetic religious traditions and spirituality movements to offer a counter-cultural way of living. Has Christianity moved from a religion in its origins for those in the underside of life to a comfortable religion of the affluent, at least in Western countries? (c.f. Metz).

Our world is dominated by science. Science makes the world go around. Computers guide planes to their destination. The Hadron Collider buried deep in the French/Swiss Alps uncovers amazing data about the beginnings of the universe. Medical science performs miracle cures and allows people to live much longer. Much of the food we eat is grown with the help of science. However, with all the genius of science, one might question whether humanity is better off emotionally, psychologically and spiritually. Science and environmental concerns are uneasy bedfellows and frequently clash with conflicting interests. Science faces ethical issues arising from such concerns as new technologies related to neuroscience, human reproduction and genetic modification. Science can explain facts but it can never explain the power of love and the quest for meaning in the human heart.

Rich and poor

The massive disparity between rich and poor has widened and stands as an indictment on world conscience. One third of the world's seven billion people live in luxury or at least in relatively comfortable material security while perhaps as many as two thirds of humanity struggle with disease and hunger, and often lack the basic necessities of life. Gandhi's observation about the disparity of wealth distribution is apt, 'The earth produces enough for everyone but not for the greed of some'. About forty-five million people are refugees living in dire poverty with little hope of settlement. Each day, 15,000 children die from hunger or diseases related to drinking polluted water. The gap between rich and poor is widening because the increment in population, estimated to be about nine billion in 2070, is largely happening in the poorest countries of the world. Even more disturbing than the data about the population expanding exponentially is the widespread culture of greed and corruption among some of those in leadership roles in the international financial markets.

Social cohesion

The speed of social change has accelerated the breakdown of traditional family structures causing havoc in family patterns and community shared values for the common good. The traditional form of family as father, mother and children has become transformed into a complex mix of blended families, cohabitation, rising incidence of divorce and separation, reproductive technologies and a growing movement towards same-sex unions. In New Zealand, half of all children are born out of wedlock. In France, the number is slightly higher at 52%. Media images of the 'ideal' body places relentless pressure on young people to conform to a stereotype of the 'ideal body'. Millions of migrants and displaced people are wandering from country to country, living in serious deprivation and desperately seeking refuge. An increasingly secularised society is a barren spiritual wasteland in offering only commerce as a way of happiness. A secularised culture never promotes a vision for life that reaches into the spiritual hearts of its people. A cult of individualism contradicts a communal commitment to the common good.

Evolving religious moments

One of the more significant cultural happenings in the 21st century will be the promotion of inter-faith dialogue. Already the manifestations of inter-faith dialogue are evident in religious gatherings and conversations. The Sufi poet and mystic Rumi (13th century) described the different religions of his time as, 'The lamps are different but the light is the same, it comes from the beyond'. Faced with a growing ethic of crass materialism and threats to planetary wellbeing, humankind is being called back to its deep spiritual roots in the human psyche.

Religious traditions are enriched by a 'passing over' to enter the wisdoms of other traditions. The experience of 'passing over' involves an attentive listening to how other religious traditions understand their own truth. According to

Raimon Panikkar, a Catholic priest and Hindu scholar, and one of the most eminent proponents of inter-faith dialogue, 'He who knows only his own religion, doesn't know his own religion'.

For thousands of years, people have sought meaning in the face of the mysteries of life and death through worship, rituals and beliefs. For ancient people, the unseen world was alive with spiritual energy. Early peoples personalised these unseen spirits and worshipped the spirits in the wind, trees, mountains and rivers. The sense of the 'numinous' (Rudolf Otto) is a feature of all religions. Primal religious practices were closely interwoven with nature and seasonal rhythms. Religions of an animism character believed that the spirits were everywhere and explained everything that happened. Nature religions expressed their relationships to divine spirits in art, rock carvings and symbolic stories. Formal religions evolved within an archaic, magical and polytheist era.

About 5000 years ago, formal religions began to appear especially in Egypt, India and other Eastern lands. Hinduism and Buddhism evolved 2000 years before Christ. Judaism became more defined as a religion about 3000 years ago. Most religions evolve out of earlier religions and doctrines. Buddhism emerged out of Hinduism. Christianity emerged out of Judaism. Islam was born out of Judaism and Christianity. Sikhism developed from Hinduism and Islam. Baha'ism had its genesis in Christianity and Islam. What is important to remember is that the evolution of religion is a multi-facet happening, interwoven with politics, economics, ethnic identities, regional and cultural nationalism. Most people who adhere to a religious tradition are born into that tradition.

Formal religions offer their people a regularised framework to encounter a divine presence. The strength of religions is communal cohesion, establishing a viable meaning vision for life and an ethical system. A potential (and historically real) weakness of religion is minimising personal encounters with the mystery of the divine presence. The danger for religions is to separate people from adult personal experiences of God and reinforce the exclusive power of intermediaries between the divine and the people. In the Christian story, the sharp division between clergy and laity for most of its history well illustrates the problem for religions. The *Catholic Encyclopaedia* of 1914 stated, 'the laity are not the depositaries of spiritual power; they are the flock confided to the care of the shepherds (clergy)'.

Contemporary spiritualities

When the dynamics of society change, so does religious affiliation. Religion is a unifying factor in the social cohesion of a society. Rapid change in the character of society is being experienced in many Western countries. Such a change in the cultural mores affects the power of religions to be a force for social cohesion. After World War II, there was an immense dispersion of religious traditions through post-war migration and more recently internet technology has given people access to a diversity of religious traditions. Today there are growing movements of spiritual guides who share diverse beliefs rather than beliefs associated with specific religious traditions. Raimon Panikkar describes how the theme of a Universal Spirit pervades the whole of creation. In his concept of a 'cosmotheandric vision of reality', Panikkar proposes that there are three irreducible dimensions of reality, the divine (*theos*), humanity (*anthropos*) and the creation of the universe (*cosmos*). According to Panikkar, all revelation about the Divine Energy or Universal Spirit emerges out of the interaction between these three dimensions of reality.

Historians of religions, such as Karen Armstrong, believe we are now entering a second Axial period for religion. The first great Axial period happened between 800 and 200 BCE where the enduring traditions of Confucianism and Taoism in China, Hinduism and Buddhism in India, monotheism in Israel and the philosophical rationalism in Greece flourished. The first Axial period was an era of major transformation of religion and people's awareness of their inner world.

According to Armstrong and other historians of religion, it would seem that a second Axial period has been slowly emerging since the 16th century. The second axial period is characterised by religious pluralism, global awareness, ecological connectedness, demise of patriarchy and a new spiritual awakening. Global technology has enabled people to have access to other people's culture and religious traditions. Indigenous religious wisdoms of North American Indian tribes, Maori and Australian Aborigines are now better known and appreciated. Never before has there been such a cross fertilisation of ideas and movements of religion through migration and international travel. Such a movement challenges those religions which hold exclusive claims about their claim to a monopoly of truth in their religious beliefs (Kirkwood: 8).

Paradoxically, the rise of fundamentalism is a feature of the second Axial period because the very idea of religious pluralism is anathema to those who make claims to hold absolute truths. Fundamentalists have no hesitation in using violence to counter the threat of people making different choices about their religious affiliation. There has been a steady increase of overt attacks on Christians in countries such as China, India, Nigeria, Sri Lanka, Iraq and Israel. There is also a more subtle, but no less insidious threat to religious freedom through legal impositions by the state. Another feature of the second axial period is the splintering of religions. At the last count, there were 38,000 different Christian groups.

As a contrast to the slow evolution of the second great axial period in the development of religion, there is a growing secularism and aggressive atheism. The New Atheism movement considers religion as a kind of superstitious relic from the past which will disappear as people become scientifically educated. A serious threat to the vitality of religions in consumer orientated societies is the 'commodity' culture which erodes a sense of the spiritual. Consumerism spawns a 'commodity' mindset. A 'commodity' culture propagates the idea that everything can be reduced to a 'commodity'. A 'commodity' culture induces a kind of consumerist torpor which limits religious imagination and the ascetical demands of Christian discipleship.

The nature of religions is to go beyond the exterior and 'commodity' mindset and journey to the inner depths of humanity where the divinity resides. Buddhism teaches that the three great poisons for humanity are greed, ill will and delusion. Each of these 'poisons' is the fruit of an inner loss of meaning. When the Spirit is shrivelled up by suffocating consumerism, a person tries to substitute a 'commodity' in order to fulfil a yearning for meaning. Where one lives, what one wears, an attractive appearance, social status, the work one does, all such externals become the driving force to find personal meaning. A 'commodity' culture which is devoid of a spiritual centre becomes a kind of treadmill of life events without ultimate meaning.

Another significant movement in contemporary religions is the increased emphasis placed on 'inner' religion rather than 'outer' religion. 'Inner religion' is more interested in meditation, general spirituality, connectedness with the divine presence, planetary relationships, interiority and individual quest for spiritual enlightenment. 'Outer religion' highlights public worship, doctrines, canon law and explicit membership to a religious tradition. 'Inner' and 'outer' religions are not opposites. They are complementary. However, the 'outer' must always be energised by the 'inner'. Contemplation is an integral feature of 'inner' religious experience.

Although affiliation with traditional religions such as Christianity, is losing ground in Western countries there is an upsurge in matters relating to spirituality. Studies of the brain show that human nature is wired for spirituality (c.f. Zohar & Marshall). Many religions hold that the *imago Dei* or 'image of God' or Divine Source lies in the deepest recesses of our being. Spirituality at its core implies a quest to encounter the divine through seeking a union with the essential Energy of life. The Latin word is *spiritus* meaning 'breath'. Until recently, spirituality for most Christians was linked with participation in

Church worship and devotions. Today, the concept of spirituality has broadened to embrace both personal and communal expressions of multiple pathways to encounter a divine Energy. The rich traditions of Eastern spiritualities, especially Buddhism and Hinduism, as well as indigenous spiritualities, have enriched the treasures of Christian spiritualities. The Universal Spirit moves across the globe. The very diversity of spiritualities invites people to dialogue and celebrate the wisdoms of each tradition.

Ecological awareness

Since the late 20th century, global ecological awareness has become more attuned to the reality of a looming ecological crisis. Through a rapid global expansion of industrialised emissions, climate change is being accelerated with a consequent fallout for species survival and increment in natural disasters. A majority of scientists agree that human activity, especially in the increased use of fossil fuels, has contributed to the warming of the globe. A recent study of oceans and marine ecosystems showed that 70% to 90% of coral in the Indian ocean and 25% of coral worldwide perished in the marine temperature spike in 1998 (Roberts: Ocean of Life). The small island of Kirbati in central Pacific with its population of just over 100,000 will probably be the first country to be drowned this century as a result of global warming.

World populations have dramatically increased from about one billion in 1650 to two billion in 1900, seven billion in early 21st century and a projected nine billion by the end of the 21st century. The great majority of the world population lives in crowded cities with minimal direct contact with nature. A teacher friend shared with me her disbelief when some inner city children on an excursion to a farm were amazed to see milk coming from cows. They believed milk was manufactured in a factory. An Australian study found that 25% of Australian children had never been on a bush walk nor climbed a tree while 17% of children had never visited a national park (*Courier Mail* June 27, 2012). A growing ecological awareness has been augmented by learning from the wisdoms of indigenous people about our inherent connectedness with nature. After observing the onward movement of settlers expanding westwards across the USA plains in the 19th century, Chief Seattle lamented, 'This we know. The Earth does not belong to man; man belongs to the earth. This we know. All things are connected like blood which unites one family. Whatever befalls the Earth, befalls the sons of the earth. Man did not weave the web of life; he is merely a strand in it. Whatever he does to the web, he does to himself'.

Mechanistic scientific theories about nature became popular during the late 17th century onwards. Newton's Laws of motion (1687) viewed the earth as like an enormous machine that followed predictable laws of physics. The philosopher Rene Descartes (1596-1650) postulated that matter was inert and only in humans did the mind exist. His famous dictum, *cogito ergo sum* (Latin: 'I think therefore I am') separated out the rational self from the rest of the universe. Mechanistic theories of the natural laws provided a rationale for the pillaging of the earth. The scientist Francis Bacon (1561-1626) once wrote that nature is to be 'tortured' until it yields up its secrets. Ancient beliefs held that natural things had an inner life (see Aristotle). Such beliefs were discarded as incompatible with a scientific view of the world. However, the scientific view of the world which expanded rapidly after the seventeenth century, also inaugurated an extraordinary array of scientific inventions which brought untold benefits to our modern world.

During the 20th century, new theories of science contradicted mechanistic laws of physics. Quantum physics proposed that all things in creation are interrelated and interconnected. In the early 20th century, the physicist David Bohm proposed a theory about the dynamics of the universe. Bohm's theory postulated that there were two levels in the order of the universe, the 'explicate order' and the 'implicate order'. Bohm named external things like ethnic groups and nations as 'explicate order' while 'implicate order' is a deep unifying order which brings an underlying unity to the basic energies of creation. The 'implicate order' may be considered as a common or collective consciousness. Christians might choose to name the 'implicate order' as the creative Spirit, Divine Energy or the power of Divine Love.

There is an essential oneness in matter which is always in transition moving through phases of birth, chaos, reconstruction and evolution. What is a matter of grave concern for planetary wellbeing is that humans now possess the technological power to alter dramatically the dynamism of natural selection. For billions of years, natural selection of species and genetic mutation happened naturally. Now humans have developed technology which empowers them to determine who survives and who dies. According to Swimme and Tucker, *cultural selection has overwhelmed natural selection* (101). The new era in the story of the relationship between humanity and the earth has been called the 'anthropocene' ('man made') era because humans can now shape the natural system by technology. There have been five mass extinctions during the last 500 million years and it seems we are now entering the prospect of a sixth mass extinction. It takes millions of years to recover from mass extinctions.

Gender equity

During the late 19th and 20th centuries, there was a gradual shift in thinking about gender issues and a critique of patriarchy ('father rule') in society and church. Scientific research (e.g. the research of Karl Ernst Van Baer in 1827) demonstrated the fallacy of a traditional male belief about his unique physical role in conception in contrast to the purported passivity of the woman's role. Taboos against women through purity laws related to the menstrual period persist in some culture even in present times. One of the reasons for excluding women from priestly ministry was related to blood flows from their monthly period.

By the late 20th century, equity between men and women was enshrined by law in Western countries. By 2016, it is estimated that 70% of all university graduates globally will be women. However, patriarchy still rules supreme in some cultures and in religions such Catholic and Orthodox Church and Islam. God is neither female nor male and beyond gender. Patriarchy has its basis in historical ignorance of human biology. The Christian ideal of gender inclusion is summed up by Paul, *There is no longer Jew or Greek, there is no longer slave or free, there is no longer male or female; for all of you are one in Christ Jesus* (Galatians 3:28).

Christian theology was deeply influenced by a Greek philosopher Aristotle (384-322 BCE) who wrote, *And a woman is as it were an infertile male; the female, in fact, is female on account of inability of a sort...The male provides the "form" and the "principle of the movement", the female provides the body, in other words, the material...* (*on the genesis of the creatures.* Bk 1 Ch 20). The most influential Christian theologian, Thomas Aquinas wrote, *In higher animals, brought into being through coitus, the active power resides in the male's semen, as Aristotle says, while the material of the foetus is provided by the female* (*Summa Theologica* 1a 118,1 ad 4).

The rationale for still upholding patriarchal structures in the Church simply does not stand up to serious historical scrutiny in contemporary consciousness. A Church with entrenched patriarchal structure in its ministry has less and less credibility in cultures which legally and socially uphold gender equity. The inclusive community of Jesus stands at variance with an embedded patriarchal church culture which excludes women from the highest levels of official Church governance and presiders of the Eucharist. It is quite extraordinary that one of the reasons given for the non-ordination of women is that a priest is an *alter Christus* or 'another Christ'. Because Christ was male, therefore a priest must be male. According to that kind of logic, every priest in the world would have to be a circumcised Jew! In any case, 'Christ' is neither male nor female but the living iconic manifestation of God beyond the physicality of gender. For a woman to become 'another Christ' she does not have to become a male! Consider, *if anyone is in Christ there is a new creation* (2 Corinthians

5:18). We also recall the words of St Cyprian of Carthage (martyred in 258), *Christianus alter Christus* (every Christian is another Christ').

Emerging consciousness

The story of the evolution of the human species and the evolution of consciousness has been discussed earlier in the text. Mention has already been made about how science has tended to focus on the external manifestations of evolution, such as biology and physics. What about the interior cultural world of evolution? According to Phipps, *If we want to fully understand the nature of evolution, and especially cultural evolution, consciousness is where the keys are* (171).There is evidence that humanity is breaking through to another leap in a new level of consciousness, a 'Cosmic 'consciousness. Evolution seems to move along with very slow changes and then suddenly leaps into a new level of consciousness. All the evidence seems to point to humankind now experiencing such a sudden leap!

The Jesuit priest and palaeontologist Pierre Teilhard de Chardin saw a continuous evolutionary upwards movement of the human spirit from 'cosmogenesis' to 'noosgenesis' to the 'Omega Point' with the Cosmic Christ as the culmination of human consciousness. The era of emerging consciousness is a journey of discovering larger horizons for humanity, especially in reconnecting humanity with its earthly roots. I have discussed earlier in the text the emergence of this transpersonal consciousness. By embracing mutli-disciplinary approaches to new knowledge and spiritual wisdoms, global communications through technology and conversations with peers, it seems that an increasing number of people are moving towards a deepened level of consciousness (O'Murchu 84-86). The trigger for such a shift in a higher level of consciousness may be related to specific crisis in cultural upheavals such as the Reformation (16th century), the French revolution, the two World Wars, cosmology, ecological crisis and the cyber revolution.

One interesting aspect of our understanding of emerging communal consciousness is the growth of scientific interest in the theory of 'morphic resonance'. The concept of 'morphic resonance' has been discussed earlier in the book. By 'morphic resonance' we mean how an individual organism can be influenced by the behaviour of other organisms of the same species despite having no physical contact with them (Macgregor: 65). The biologist Rupert Sheldrake, proposed this theory about the interaction between energy fields. According to Sheldrake, every species has a species-specific morphic field that determines its social and cultural systems. All humans, for example, have the capacity to influence others through their specific human morphic field. Our good deeds and positive energy can, and do, generate positive energy in others, even those who may be far away. Our very humanity has a common base of connectedness. As explained earlier, although Sheldrake's theory has not been verified by other scientific studies, it seems to be authenticated by popular human experiences relating to the common good.

The implications of the reality of morphic resonance for human behaviour and spiritual development are enormous. Positive initiatives for justice and earth care impact on others who may be far from the specific location of the initial actions. Prayers for others travel through morphic energy fields to transmit love and support. The proclamation of the Good News can move through energy fields into communal consciousness. The sufferings, death and resurrection of Jesus who became the Christ become a universal redemptive act through morphic resonance which, for Christians, pertains to a belief in the Universal Christ.

'Signs of the times' and hope

In seeking to highlight some features of the 'signs of the times' as a context for telling the evolutionary story of Christianity, two issues need to be noted.

First, it would give a distorted picture of 'signs of the times' if the picture of social and religious trends seems to be one of 'gloom and doom'. Research on social attitudes indicates that the majority of people are moderately content with their lives and get on with living, making the best of opportunities. There are countless examples of generosity, kindness and goodness expressed in communities every day. For every one social aberration reported by the media in news bulletins, there are hundreds of unreported events of community service, family love and caring relationships. According to an ancient saying, *amor est diffisivum sui* (Latin: 'love spreads itself everywhere). The power and energy of love is a reminder that there is an abundance of God's love and compassion being manifest every day in the world. For every reported clerical abuse, there are millions of examples of Christian service that give hope, sustenance, justice and love to people all over the world.

Secondly, it must be emphasised again that the 'signs of the times' described here are a random selection of some issues in Western countries which impact on the Christian story. If one were describing 'signs of the times' in countries such as Singapore, Papua New Guinea, South Africa, Syria, Sudan or Mongolia, there would be different pressing issues in some of these countries such as, AIDS, ethnic violence, famine, widespread corruption in government, family cohesion, religious intolerance, poverty, tribalism and so on. Issues of faith that preoccupy many in the West about the life of the church may not even register with people of other countries. However, I do believe that some of the 'signs of the times' such as globalisation, disparity of wealth, gender issues, spirituality, dominance of capitalism are relevant in virtually every country.

Conclusion

This chapter has discussed a selection of topics on the cultural landscape and the need to recognise the 'signs of the times'. The art of recognising the 'signs of the times' necessitates compassionate listening, being involved in the ordinary happenings of people's lives, discerning, researching and sharing the wisdoms of a wide circle of people. Obstacles to reading the 'signs of the times' include blocks such as spiritual arrogance, being remote from people's lives, ignorance of modern life issues and a disinclination to engage in discerned listening. Social commentators suggest that our world is in a state of rapid transition which invites both challenges and opportunities for the gospel.

If the Genesis origin myth is interpreted as a symbolic story about the evolution of the human species, then those telling the Christian story will be attentive listeners to the heartbeats of unfolding world culture. According to an ancient Christian saying, 'the place of reality is the invitation to grace'. Grace awaits people of faith in every phase of life. God did not create the world and then abandon it to its fate. Those who see the possibilities of the gospel to transform culture and make the world a more harmonious place will leave no stone unturned to become aware of the 'signs of the times' and respond accordingly.

In the next chapter, we will consider the Jesus story and the Christian community on its evolutionary journey of Emergence.

CHAPTER SEVEN

The Christian story within an emergence vision

This chapter brings us to the heart of the theme of this book. In the light of evolutionary science, who is Jesus as the Christ and how might the Christian story be told in today's world? Is there a different perspective on the Christ story from the more traditional Fall/redemption theme if the story is told from an Emergence rather than a Fall context?

Who is Jesus?

If the Genesis origin myth is interpreted as a symbolic story about the beginning of the long evolutionary journey of human consciousness in an evolving world, questions such as the following arise about Jesus the Christ and the Christian community,

Who is Jesus who became the Christ and what does the incarnation mean?'
What does the Christ story mean in the evolution of global consciousness?

How does the Christian community continue to proclaim the revelation of God in Jesus? How might the Christian community cooperate with other great religious traditions to promote the wellbeing of humanity and creation?

How might an evolutionary perspective on the mission of the Christian community shape the way the church actually engages in its mission?

Jesus, Yeshua bar Josef, was probably born in Nazareth in about the year of 4 BCE. Nazareth was a tiny hilltop town in northern Palestine which had come under Roman rule in 63 BCE. Jesus grew up as a pious Jew with his parents Joseph, Mary and his brothers and sisters. About the age of thirty, Jesus went to the desert and experienced a profound religious experience. After he emerged from the desert he began to preach his message of the Kingdom of God. Most of his preaching and healing were around the lake of Galilee and its region with the town of Capernaum as his base. In the Jewish tradition of charismatic teachers, his dynamic preaching and healing soon began to attract large crowds. However, his popularity aroused the hostility of the powerbrokers among the religious caste and they soon began to plot his death (Mark 3:6). A community of disciples gathered around Jesus to share and proclaim the Good News of the Kingdom.

After perhaps only three short years, the growing popularity of Jesus provoked the religious authorities to ally themselves with the hated Roman military to end the threat to their religious power. Jesus was captured and executed in about 30 CE. Following his death, God raised Jesus up as the Christ. The previously dispersed disciples now reassembled and, inspired by the Spirit, began to fearlessly preach the Good News. The new religious movement, soon to be called Christianity, quickly spread throughout the Roman Empire and the wider world.

During the last 2000 years, Christianity has emerged as a major religious and cultural movement spanning almost every country across the globe. Currently, just over 30% of the seven billion people in the world are Christian. Christian culture and services are almost universal in their scope especially in education, welfare and health.

As explained earlier in the book, 'Christ' is not the surname of Jesus. 'Christ' is a title meaning 'the anointed one' and refers to the 'anointing' of Jesus by the Spirit. 'Christ' is an expression of the manifestation of God in the whole of creation.

Who is Jesus and what was his mission?

If we accept an interpretation of the Genesis origin myth as a symbolic story about the beginning of humankind's evolutionary journey, what is the role of Jesus as the Christ in this evolutionary journey?

The question *Cur Deus Homo* ('why did God become a man'), posed by Anselm in 1098, has been an abiding question in Christology through the ages, especially during and after theological debates of the 11th century. A traditional answer to that question has been that God became man in the person of Jesus to redeem humanity from the sin inherited from our first parents. In other words, the dominant theme in explaining the mission of Jesus was that his suffering and death secured our redemption. Redemption theology has been the standard explanation for the mission of Jesus for much of Christian history.

If we accept that there was no such a thing as a Fall, at least in the way the Genesis origin myth was interpreted, then the traditional explanation for the mission of Jesus is no longer adequate. The Christ event is not a backward looking belief about rectifying a purported moral failure in the mists of time. Rather, the Christ event is a forward looking vision for the possibilities of humanity and all of creation, *He is the image of the invisible God, the first born of all creation; for in him were created all things in heaven and on earth, visible and invisible... He himself is before all things, and in him all things hold together* (Colossians 1:15-17).

Incarnation

The central belief of Christianity is encapsulated in John 1:14, *And the Word became flesh and lived among us.* The incarnation expresses the generativity of God who is love (1 John 4:16). The Divine Energy, who has breathed life into the universe (Genesis 1:2), is the underlying energy of creation and love. All true love wishes to express and share love. A Divine Energy of Love who brought all creation into being, longs for love to be reciprocated. God created humans in God's own image and likeness so that God could share and receive love in caring relationships. Jesus was born into the world as a manifestation of the fruits of God's generativity. For a Christian, Jesus exemplifies in human terms the nature of God.

Christians believe that Jesus as the Christ is a fusion of the divine Presence and humanity. Jesus who became the Christ is God's love in flesh. Women and men are created in the image and likeness of God (Genesis 1:27). The 14th century mystic Juliana of Norwich wrote, *The human soul was made to be God's dwelling place.* Through the incarnation, Jesus who became the Christ, embarked on his mission to reveal to humanity the fullness and wonder of being created in God's image. His mission was to enhance the deification of humans within the oneness of creation. God became a person so that we might become like God (deification).

One of the very early Church Fathers, St Irenaeus of Lyons (d c 200) once wrote, *The Word of God, our Lord Jesus Christ, who did, through his transcendent love became what we are that he might bring us to be even what he is himself* (Adversus Haereses 5). St Athanasius (d 373) wrote that, *God became man so that we might become deified* (Migne, *Patrologia Graeca*, 25,192 B De Incarnatione Verbi, 54). As Jesus shared our humanity, we too share his divinity as the risen Christ. Jesus epitomises the possibility of an incarnation in every single person. One of the first followers of St Francis of Assisi, St Bonaventure (1221-1274), wrote, 'You exist more truly where you love than where you live since you are transformed into the likeness of whatever you love through the power of love itself'.

To speak about the saving and redemptive mission of Jesus is to describe how people may be made more whole. Salvation is not an after death event as a reward for a good life. Salvation refers to a bringing someone into healing and wholeness, integrating body, mind and spirit. The core message of Jesus is explicitly stated in John 10:10, *I came that they may have life, and have it abundantly.* God is a God of life. As Saviour and Redeemer, Jesus' mission was to lead people beyond sin to a fullness of life. The theme of 'abundance of life' is **the** mantra for all Christian living, abundance of life for self, others and creation. One can always evaluate the authenticity of Christian teaching and living if these teachings enhance the wellbeing of people and creation.

Reign of God

The central message of Jesus was the 'reign of God'. Again and again, this message is reiterated and described in sayings and parables. Richard Rohr described the 'reign of God' as 'the Big Picture'. The image of the reign of God was the Dream of Jesus for a time of peace, harmony and justice for all people when God's gracious love would become a reality. In transpersonal consciousness, the image of the reign of God portrays a time when God's love and compassion embraces the whole world. Jesus was passionately committed to his proclamation, *I came to bring fire to the earth and how I wish it were already kindled* (Luke 12:49). His teachings sought to liberate people from oppressions (Luke 4:16-21) so that they might be free to encounter a gracious God. He also challenged excessive impositions of religious authorities that stifled religious experiences. Jesus taught about the abundance of grace not its scarcity.

Although Jesus as a faithful Jew revered his heritage and traditions, he did not hesitate to subvert those aspects of traditional thinking which denied people their inherent dignity. In his ministry Jesus was prepared to reverse the order of social standing by announcing, *So the last will be first, and the first will be last* (Matthew 20:16). In contrast to prevailing cultural views about women among some Jewish groups of a patriarchal society, Jesus affirmed the dignity of women. The Samaritan woman at Jacob's well (John 4), Mary of Bethany who anointed Jesus, Martha and Mary in Bethany, Mary his mother and other women figure prominently in the ministry of Jesus. It is a woman, Mary Magdalene, who was the one chosen to tell the disciples the wonderful news of the resurrection (John 20:17). The reign of God proclaimed a new era where traditional social and religious barriers were dismantled. How could the model of compassion be a hated Samaritan (Luke 10:30-36)? Why was the younger son, not the elder son, rewarded with the symbol of authority (Luke 15:11-32)?

Jesus paid scant attention to the trappings of religion. He taught a **way** of living, not a series of doctrines about religion. He abhorred the hypocrisy of those religious leaders who emphasised the format of religion instead of its religious heart (Matthew 23:13-16). Jesus caused mayhem in the temple by driving out sellers and buyers, overturned money tables and seats of those selling doves, crying out, *'My house shall be called a house of prayer; but you are making it a den of robbers* (Matthew 21:31).

Jesus and justice

If there was one theme in the ministry of Jesus that was paramount, it was his passionate commitment to justice. In response to the question from John the Baptist about his identity, Jesus replied, *Go and tell John what you hear and see; the blind receive their sight, the lame walk, the lepers are cleansed, the deaf hear, the dead are raised, and the poor have good news brought to them* (Matthew 11:4). In other words, you will know who I am through my caring relationships with the dispossessed.

According to Luke, Jesus begins his public ministry in his home town Nazareth by reading from the scroll in the synagogue and quoting from Isaiah about letting the oppressed go free (Luke 4:17-21). He then added the provocative statement, *Today this scripture has been fulfilled in your hearing* (21). In the scene of the Last Judgment, the only criterion for living the gospel authentically is specified as responding to the needs of the marginalised, *for I was hungry and you gave me food, or thirsty and you gave me something to drink, I was a stranger and you welcomed me, I was naked and you gave me clothing, I was sick and you took care of me, I was in prison and you visited me* (Matthew 25:35-36). Using the imagery of Matthew, one can always test the authenticity of one's spirituality by observing a person's commitment to justice and the common good. Gospel spirituality is liberation theology in action.

The principle of the common good is not some abstract philosophical principle but grounded actions towards justice. According to Aristotle, justice is the most perfect virtue because it orientates human actions towards the wellbeing of others. The sins of people and structural sins are not sins against God but a failure to work for caring and liberating relationships with others. It is no coincidence that one of the most repeated injunctions of Jesus was his insistence on reconciliation (Matthew 5:23). The incidence of human trafficking, domestic violence, famine, ethnic discrimination, ecological vandalism, greed, racism and countless other aberrations, all cry out for compassionate responses. Everyone is challenged to utilise their birth-gifts to alleviate suffering. St Teresa of Avila (1515-1582) reminds us that the mercy of God can only happen when we ourselves actually engage in working for justice. She wrote, 'Christ has no body now but yours; no hands, no feet on earth but yours. Yours are the eyes through which he looks with compassion on the world. Christ has nobody on earth but you'.

God in the ordinary

The teachings of Jesus reflect his very ordinariness by being with people in their life situations. He told stories about farmers sowing crops, travellers, housewives, fishermen, birds looking for food, tax collectors, lilies in the fields, disobedient children, weddings and unjust stewards. As a child growing up in Nazareth, he never lost the common touch with ordinary people. By grounding his teachings in everyday happenings, Jesus wished to highlight that God is present in the very banal things of life. As Paula D'Arcy would say, 'God comes to us disguised as our life'. The incarnation reminds Christians that there are not two realms of reality. The spiritual and material are one in God's sight. Humans have evolved in their own unique way from the long chain of life forms in the earth.

Learn to trust in God's providence, said Jesus, just look at God's providential care in nature, *Consider the ravens, they neither sow nor reap, they have neither storehouse nor barn, and yet God feeds them... Consider the lilies, how they grow: they neither toil nor spin; yet I tell you, even Solomon in all his glory, was not clothed like one of these* (Luke 12:24, 27).

Jesus the holy one

Jesus taught about prayer and moral living. His intimacy with God is manifest in addressing God as *Abba* or loving Father. He insisted that grace is for everyone, not just for a chosen few. In his teachings, he kept proclaiming that God is a God of compassion and mercy, not a remote judge. As a Spirit person, he went into the desert to discern his vocation (Matthew 4:1-11). At his baptism in the river Jordan, Jesus experienced the overwhelming sense of being God's beloved son, *You are my Son the Beloved; with you I am well pleased* (Mark 1:11). Jesus nourished his life by daily prayer. The gospels record his long nights in prayer. Jesus prayed when he cured the sick and cast out demons. He taught us about the indwelling of God in us, *On that day you will know that I am in my Father, and you are in me and I am in you* (John 14:20).

The sufferings and the death of Jesus

The suffering and death of Jesus was a traumatic event for his family and disciples. His disciples asked, 'How could this happen?' Why did it happen?' New Testament writers sought answers to this dilemma by drawing from their Jewish sources and proposing various theories related to a ransom or atonement rationale. These explanations have been discussed earlier. Such explanations do not sit easily with contemporary consciousness. Jesus did not interpret his death as some kind of sacrificial atonement offered to the Father (Pagola: 354). Jesus could never imagine that his loving Father would ever desire a violent death for his Beloved Son. God had no need of a sacrificial offering to atone for sin. God's gracious love is always present with unconditional forgiveness.

The cross was not a payment due to God's demand for reparation but an intentional act by Jesus to accept the consequences of absolute fidelity to his mission. The cross stands as a poignant symbol of solidarity with all the suffering in the world and the awful price paid for confronting evil and sin. Standing near the cross of Jesus were not only his mother, some women and the beloved disciple (John 19:25) but the universal assembling of all those suffer, the victims of famine, AIDS and ethnic cleansing, the persecuted, refugees, the socially marginalised and abused. The cross is a terrible testimony of what violent people sometimes do to one another. The story of the Lutheran pastor Dietrich Bonhoeffer is a story of pathos to illustrate the mindless violence of evil people. He returned from USA to his native country Germany to confront Nazi tyranny. He denounced the Nazis and was hung on 10 April 1945. His letters from prison spoke about 'costly grace', a horrific price to pay for his fidelity to his mission.

We cannot escape the vagaries of life. Everything in creation is part of a recurring cycle of birth-death-rebirth. Death is not a punishment of some primal moral failing but an integral facet of evolution. Indigenous people in Australia have known for thousands of years that they must do selected burning of grasslands for the regeneration of new pastures to safeguard the sustainability of the land. For Christians, the cross symbol encourages people to face 'failure' situations and look for ways of learning from mistakes to transform setbacks in life. Carl Jung wrote how the shadow of each person contains energy which can be utilised for growth. The shadow can also lead to despair if unaddressed or projected on to others. In one of his songs, Leonard Cohen sings, 'There is a crack in everything. That is how the light gets in'.

Jesus had no problems with 'failures' in his interactions with people. Instead, he called 'failure' people into new pathways of growth. Suffering and failures are primary teachers of life if they become steps in personal transformations. Unresolved hurts poison relationships. Peacemakers strive to transform rejections into opportunities for personal and communal growth. The cross is an invitation to 'grace' or 'break' – a grace for transformation or a burden to be endured. In Holy Week liturgy, Christians celebrate the 'Pascal Mystery' where the agony of the cross on Good Friday is followed by rolling away the stone to resurrection on Easter Sunday (Luke 24:2).

Resurrection

The death of Jesus was not the end but a passage into the transformation of the resurrection. The resurrection was not a resuscitation of a corpse. The resurrection was not a physical event but a spiritual happening. Through the resurrection, Jesus moves beyond historical time into the eternal time of Christ. If the bones of Jesus were unearthed somewhere in the previous land of Palestine, it should not make the slightest differences to beliefs about the resurrection. Jesus was raised by God as the Christ into a glorified being or in the words of Mark, *another form* (16:12). St Paul is explicit about the centrality of the resurrection to the Christian faith, *and if Christ has not been raised, then our proclamation has been in vain and your faith has been in vain* (1 Corinthians 15:14).

The resurrection is the vindication of God's power to give meaning to death. According to the Fall tradition, death is a consequence of the sin of Adam and Eve (Genesis 3:3, 19). Death can feel like entering the nothingness of the great unknown. Most humans have an innate dread of death and fear of facing the after-death time. Even Jesus, facing his imminent death, cried out in terror and fell to the ground in the Gethsemane, praying in desperation, *Father, if you are willing, remove this cup from me* (Luke 22: 42). Jesus did not die in emptiness but in absolute trust in God, *Then Jesus, crying in a loud voice, said, 'Father, into your hands, I commend my spirit'. Having said this he breathed his last* (Luke 23:46). The resurrection is the apex in the story of Jesus as Christ. Paul's writings and the recorded speeches in the Acts focus on the resurrection as the turning point of the Christ event (Ephesians 1:12-14; Acts 2:32).

The resurrection stories in the gospels are characterised by feeling of unbounded joy and wonder from the disciples (Luke 24:52). Their despair is dispelled by the light of the resurrected Christ. The focus of the redemptive mission of Christ was not about making up to God for our sins but offering a new wondrous vision for the transformed life, a *life in abundance*. The resurrection celebrated death as entering a new phase in our evolutionary journey of life (Delio 2011:95-96). Death is a passage time to a new 'resurrected' existence as a child of God. We may call this new phase of life 'heaven'.

The resurrection of Jesus as Christ is replicated by each individual person who moves from the evolutionary reality of death into new life. According to Mahoney, *In other words, the evolutionary purpose of the death of Jesus, freely undertaken, was to conduct the human species beyond individual mortality and to introduce it to the final stage of everlasting fulfilment for which it is destined by a loving God* (65). All major religions uphold traditions which affirm that at death some essential part of our being continues into another form of life.

I experienced an insight into the gospel writings about the resurrection when I saw a vision of a departed relative suspended above the gathered mourners at the burial of the ashes. His identifiable presence was shrouded in shining white clothes, gazing peacefully down upon us.

Christ in trinity

During the first four centuries of Christianity, Christians struggled to reconcile the inherited monotheism of their Jewish roots with beliefs about the divinity of Jesus as Christ. Beliefs about God as Trinity gradually were clarified at the Council of Nicea (325) and Chalcedon (451). Without delving into the complexity of theological language forms in the debates during these centuries, the metaphor of God as Trinity wishes to express something of the nature of God. The metaphor of God as Trinity speaks about God as relational, communal, self-giving, life-giving and intimately involved within all creation.

God's very being is altruistic in the generation of life. The Spirit (Hebrew: *ruach*) energises all life in the created universe (Genesis 1:2). God is the Ground of Being, the Source of love. The nature of God as Trinity is mirrored in the interdependence of all things in creation and a relational consciousness inherent in the essence of all people. Humans, imaged by the Trinity, are one and also communal by nature. Jesus spoke about the binding power of love in this relational consciousness, *By this everyone will know that you are my disciples, if you have love for one another* (John 13:35).

Christians need new language forms to express God as Trinity. To excessively intellectualise God as Trinity is to obscure its meaning. To express God as Trinity is to propose a Trinitarian God as a symbol, a poem, a musical score, a work of art, an image of Divine Communion. Perhaps Christians may be helped to better express the mystery of the oneness and diversity of God's nature by drawing from the insights of new science about the essential unity of the universe and yet its multiple manifestations. All things in the universe are interconnected, are one yet many. Most Christians simply refer to the belief of God as Trinity as a 'mystery' and leave it at that.

Language in the Nicene Creed such as, 'consubstantial', 'begotten', which were drawn from 4th century philosophical terms make no sense to people today. We also have to move beyond the polemics of gender concerns in the Trinitarian language of 'Father', 'Son' and 'Spirit' (Treston: 74). God as Trinity is an evocative imaginative metaphor for God's relational creative nature in the whole universe and especially with the human species. What a shame that the richness of the metaphor of God as Trinity is obscured in the wilderness of archaic language! The wisdoms of other religious traditions, especially Hinduism, seek to explain the unity and diversity of God's nature. Hinduism expresses the godhead which is one and yet expressed in three concepts of Brahma (creator), Vishnu (sustainer) and Shiva (destroyer).

Jesus as cosmic or universal Christ

A dilemma for Christians is holding beliefs about Christ as universal Saviour of the world and the reality that two thirds of the world's population does not believe a single word of that statement. In a pluralistic religious world, how might this apparent contradiction be reconciled?

An understanding of the mystery of the Cosmic or Universal Christ may offer a way forward to address the dilemma for Christians of belief about the Christ as universal Saviour and the reality that the majority of the world's population do not share such a belief. Jesus is the personification of Christ consciousness or the Cosmic mind. Christians believe that Christ is a universal icon for the whole of humanity and indeed all of creation (Colossians 1:15), a symbol of the divine-human unity in the universe. At the deepest level of humanity, Christians believe that the Cosmic Christ is a metaphor for the presence of the divinity within the very depths of creation (c.f. Delio 2008:173-180).

The concept of 'Cosmic Christ' or 'Universal Christ' has many names such as Krishna, Rama, Ishvara, according to diverse cultures and religious traditions. Other religious traditions have similar beliefs for a Universal Divine presence in the world and use language and metaphors that are generic to their cultural traditions. As stated above, the Hindu concept of belief goes back to its source in the Vedas (collection of hymns chanted by Brahmin priests) where the godhead is expressed in three concepts, Brahma (creator), Vishnu (sustainer)) and Shiva (destroyer). All these three concepts express various aspects of the hidden Brahma. Brahma is the Absolute, expressed as god as creator, god as sustainer and god as destroyer.

When we seek to explore the mystery of a sustaining Divine Presence in the world as expressed by the diverse religious traditions, we are drawn back to David Bohm's theory of 'implicate order' which has been previously discussed. The theory of 'implicate order' offers a possible scientific explanation for the essential and basic order keeping all things together in creation. Standing on the common ground of love, compassion, peace, reconciliation and care for the earth, all religions and spiritualities may find harmony and wellbeing.

The term 'Cosmic Christ' or 'Universal Christ' does not sit easily with most Christians, especially out of respect for the diversity of religious traditions. Christians proclaim Christ but they do not own the Cosmic Christ. Christians believe that Christ is the Universal One for all of creation. In an evolutionary appreciation of all things in creation with its growing inter-faith dialogue, a Universal Christ or Universal Krishna is an inclusive metaphor of God being in and beyond creation. The metaphor for the divine energy manifest in creation will be given other names according to beliefs of diverse religious traditions. Ramon Panikkar calls the name 'Christ' the 'Supername'. St Paul writes about the need for a new understanding of Christ, *From now on, therefore, we regard no one from a human point of view; even though we knew Christ from a human point of view, we know him no longer in that way. So if anyone is in Christ, there is a new creation, everything old has passed away, see, everything has become new* (2 Corinthians 5:16-17).

The Christian community within the perspective of emergence not fall

If we consider the Genesis origin myth as a story to illuminate the beginning of an evolutionary journey of consciousness, what are some salient implications for the life of the Christian community?

We are not proposing a new version of Christianity but shifting the focus from a Christ restoration emphasis to a Christ regeneration emphasis within an unfolding evolutionary universe.

A foundational dictum in exploring the life of the Christian community as people on an evolutionary journey of insight within the Christ story is actually to **accept** the reality of the evolutionary journey of faith and life in the Christian community. To uphold tradition and insist on scripture as God's revelation are basic to Christian faith. However, tradition or scripture alone remain disconnected without the unifying experience of a profound encounter with a living God. Unless tradition and scripture are regularly mined for new insights and new knowledge, they will gradually be relegated to isolated artefacts of a religious museum. Religions which demand obedience to language forms and worship styles that no longer connect with people's lived reality will soon suffer a diminution of affiliation.

The second aspect of Christianity in an evolutionary perspective as Emergence not Fall is being proactive in celebrating and sharing the Good News. Religion often gets a negative press. The media often highlights incidences of clergy abuse, religious fanaticism, intolerance and other aberrations. Rarely the media reports about the millions and millions of religiously motivated people who spend their lives in dedicated service to the less fortunate, who conduct welfare, education and health services, confront oppressive regimes and give compassionate leadership to communities.

From my own pastoral experiences in several countries over fifty years of ministry, I am constantly humbled and inspired by the plethora of compassionate services offered by Christian groups across the globe. Christian communities need to be much more upfront in disseminating information in the public arena about their major contributions to social cohesion and the common good. For 2000 years, Christianity has been, and is now, a major civilising influence for billions of people.

The following areas of the Christian life are worthy of renewal and discerned action.

Relationships

God created people in God's image and likeness (Genesis 1:27). By creating humans in God's image and likeness, God communicates with people in the giving and receiving love. Humans are sexual and relational by nature. The journey of spirituality is allowing the likeness and image of God to infuse one's whole being. At the depths of one's being, there is the energy of love and there, in faith, does God reside.

Using scanning devices in our brain, scientists have discovered that when a person is meditating, blood flows from the individual parts of our brain to the awareness part of our brain which is connected to relational consciousness. Unless this section of our brain is developed, we become more a prisoner of individualism and easy pickings for the addictions of consumerism. The Christian community must be a place where relational consciousness is lived and experienced. According to Jesus, *Where two or three are gathered in my name, I am there among them* (Matthew 18:20). The nurturing of relational consciousness is a prime goal for the proclamation of the gospel. Hospitality, family life, caring services, membership in a viable community, reconciliation, communal worship, a shared sense of mission, fun and laughter and networks of support, are some of the many manifestations of how relational consciousness is nurtured and experienced.

It is almost impossible to know a God of love unless we first experience love in our own lives. We recall the saying of St Augustine, 'Love and do what you will'. Within a rampant ideology of individualism in society, people are crying out for connectedness. The popularity of the social media among a younger generation is a manifestation of this desire for 24/7 connections through Facebook, iPhones and Twitter. Our sexuality reminds us that we are relational and communal in the essence of our being. Christian communities must be places where members feel that they belong, are welcomed and are invited to share their birth-gifts.

The great majority of young people in Western countries profess no real interest in matters relating to church and yet are deeply concerned about relationships. Perhaps an approach of nurturing relational consciousness might be a fruitful pathway for the proclamation of the gospel, especially to a younger generation.

Spirituality

A fostering of spirituality is helping people become attuned to God's presence in the whole of creation. When we review the history of Christian spirituality, we cannot help noting how it became the province of a selected few, a kind of elite community of 'saints'. Historically, much of the emphasis in Christian spirituality developed into a kind of contract deal with God, that is: 'I'll do my best to fulfil my religious obligations provided you, God, do the right thing for me and get me to heaven'. That type of spirituality is a business transaction: we do things for God and God in turn does things for us.

Humans are spiritual in their genetic identity in so far as they imbibe a quest for ultimate meaning. The Dominican Meister Eckhart (13th century) reminded us that spirituality is about 'subtraction' not 'addition'. We don't need to accumulate mountains of devotions, prayer wheels and retreats to grow spiritually. The process of 'subtraction' in spirituality assumes a 'letting go' of our addictions and blocks to allow God's presence to pervade our being. Contemplation offers space for God to reside. To be spiritual is to choose 'life in abundance', for self, others and creation. St Irenaeus (d c 200) captured the essence of early Christianity when he wrote, *The glory of God is the human person fully alive* (Adversus Haereses 4:34 5-7). Rather than beat our breasts about the misfortune of being born into original sin, a wholesome spirituality celebrates our birth-gifts. More people of religious belief are gradually recognising how the Universal Spirit has spoken to people across the globe. The Universal Spirit is manifest in different religious traditions and cultural wisdoms.

The Christian community possesses vast reservoirs of spiritual wisdoms and practices such as sacraments, devotions, icons, meditation, works of charity, theology, music, art, liturgical prayers and so on. These practices should become well known to all members. The Eucharist holds a special and central place in Christian worship. It is in the celebration of the Eucharist that the Christian community gathers together to share a communal meal remembering God in Christ and the Holy Spirit in our lives. The name 'Eucharist' captures the essence of the Eucharist as 'thanksgiving' (Greek) for the wondrous gift of God's love in Jesus and the Spirit. At the Last Supper, Jesus took the bread and wine and gave thanks (Luke 22:17-19). The bread and wine, symbols of God's abundance (see Jeremiah 31:12; Amos 9:13), link Christians in the Eucharist with the abundance of creation.

Wisdom living

Wisdom is the art of making life-enhancing choices. We live in a world awash with information emanating from cyber space technology. Internet, email, television, iPod and radio disseminate an avalanche of information on every possible topic. Global technology has the potential to unite us through rallying for causes of justice and raise concerns about ecological sustainability. Global technology can also divide people by abusive remarks on Twitter and Face Book as well as disseminating information about bomb making. Sexual predators are active on the social networks and trolls debase the value of social networks. Faced with information inundation, how do we discern what information makes a positive contribution to promote 'life in abundance'? How do we make sense of the hundreds of items of information that enter our mind space every day?

The art of discernment (Latin *discere*: 'to sort out') is an ancient tradition often communicated by the elders of the tribe. Discernment implies making decisions that are in accord of God's will and for the wellbeing of people and creation. Fostering a contemplative attitude orientates a person to discover God's presence in ordinary happenings of life. A Sabbath space in one's life allows the Spirit to reside there.

One of my favourite verses from the Bible speaks about allowing the Spirit to reside in the inner sanctum of our souls, *Listen! I am standing at the door, knocking; if you hear my voice and open the door, I will come in to you and eat with you, and you with* me (Revelations 3:20). Silence attunes a person to awareness. Through meditation, we learn to be silent within. All the great religious traditions insist on the practice of meditation. In my Tai'chi teaching sessions, I encourage group members to 'clear the mind of chattering monkeys'.

In the Hebrew scripture, Wisdom literature was the way of describing God's presence in the world and living according to God's law. Sophia is the icon of the Wisdom Woman (Proverbs 8:32). In Proverbs, Sophia cries out, *To you, O people, I call, and my cry is to all that live. O simple ones, learn prudence; acquire intelligence, you who lack it. Hear for I will speak noble things, and from my lips will come what is right; from my mouth will utter truth* (Proverbs 8:4-7). Contemporary culture might appropriately be designated as 'The Information Age' because of the flood of information disseminating out of cyber technology. Such a surfeit of information can overwhelm people in seeking to make wise choices about living morally. From an early age, children should be taught how to discern what information is helpful to the human spirit and what information is detrimental to human dignity and earth wellbeing.

Jesus taught a **way** of living. He did not give us a creed of beliefs. The values he lived and was prepared to die for, had their genesis in the dignity of a person created in God's image, the pursuit of the common good and the integrity of creation. The glue which holds these values together and its driving force is the power of God's love. Although the Christian community must engage positively in the wider community, it must not hesitate to be a prophetic voice in upholding core values and confronting those values which erode the common good and dignity of people.

Children of the Earth

Our evolutionary human story is part of the great evolutionary story of the universe. Living in partnership with creation honours and reverences the wonder of creation. A commitment to 'life in abundance' is a commitment to awareness of how our human life is interconnected with cosmic life. The Aboriginal poet Kevin Gilbert (d 1993) wrote:

> *I am part of every living thing,*
> *And every living thing is part of me,*
> *We are all created of this sacred earth,*
> *So everything's our sacred family.*

The English poet John Donne wrote:

> No man is an island,
> Entire of itself.
> Each is part of the main.

Every day, we aspire to see with new eyes something of the wonder of creation: a leaf, a flower, pet's eyes, colours of a sunset or the genius of an iPhone. We are in awe of how every single species in creation has some role to play in the intricate network of life, such as phytoplankton in the oceans filling the air with oxygen enabling us to breathe. Meister Eckhart wrote, 'Every single creature is full of God, and is a book about God. Every creature is a word of God'.

We wonder at the amazing diversity of life. There are 200 species of monkeys, 25,000 species of orchids. St Bonaventure described the world as a mirror which reflects the wonder of God. Humans share much of their genetic complement of the 20,000 to 25,000 genes with other species. Ninety-seven per cent of human genes are the same genetic composition as the chimpanzee. There is much evidence to support the theory that primates and modern humans shared an ancient common ancestor.

Humankind is only slowly awakening to its ecological responsibilities. Everyone is enjoined to be a proactive co-creator by doing even the 'little' things such as recycling, planting trees, responsible use of water, electricity or more demanding public commitments such as active participation in environmental lobby groups. The pursuit of eco-justice is not an option for

Christians. It is a moral imperative. As the earth cares for us through giving us oxygen, food and water and the gift of natural wonders, so we too must care for the earth. We are utterly dependent on the earth for our very existence. If the oxygen pumped out from plants, oceans and trees ceased, we would be asphyxiated in a matter of minutes. Life in the planet faces increasing threats to its health through such happenings as deforestation, salinity, depletion of fertile soils and unbridled development.

We are all children of the stars and the stars are our biological cosmic parents. It is interesting to participate in Holy Week liturgy and observe the blessing of water by the priest. Perhaps, we might become more aware that actually it is water which blesses us instead of us blessing the water. All species, including humans, have evolved from water. We cannot survive without the gift of water.

The earth is a patient teacher if only we learn to listen to her. In the book of Job we read, *But ask the animals and they will teach you; The birds of the air; and they will tell you; Ask the plants of the earth, and they will teach* you (Job 12:7-8).The Irish missionary Columbanus (543-615) once said, 'He who tramples on the world, tramples on himself'. According to the Dali Lama, *Because we all share this small planet earth, we have to learn to live in harmony and peace with each other and with nature. This is not just a dream, but a necessity. We are dependent on each other in so many ways that we can no longer live in isolated communities and ignore what is happening outside these communities, and we must share the good fortune that we enjoy ... As interdependent, therefore, we have no other choice than to develop what I call a sense of universal responsibility. Today we are a global family. What happens in one part of the world may affect us all* (Nobel Prize Lecture 11th December 1989).

Religion offers the world a soul response to the ecological crisis as well as practical actions for earth care. Interfaith relations and interfaith dialogue constitute a formidable alliance for restoring a spirituality of sustainability. The First Covenant (Genesis 9) is a sign of eternal promise between God, humans and creation. In the Epistle to the Romans, St Paul links the Christ event with the whole of creation, *We know that the whole of creation has been groaning in labor pains until now; and not only the creation but we ourselves, who have the first fruits of the spirit* (8:22-23).

In the Genesis Origin myth, one of the most misunderstood verses in the whole Bible has been Genesis 1:28, *fill the earth and subdue it; and have dominion over... every living thing that moves upon the earth.* During the late 20th century there has been a rising consciousness that we must recover the lost art of living **with** earth rather than 'subduing' the earth or 'dominating' the earth. Humans are called to be responsible stewards, not masters of the earth.

Recovering the art of living **with** the earth involves a radical change of heart and mind, a conversion or *metanoia*, a turning around of the way we live and use the resources of the earth. Humans are members of an earth community where all species have rights within that community. The intuition of animals and their relationships with humans is well known. There is a moving story of elephants and their relationship with their great protector, a South African Lawrence Anthony. Anthony was a legend across the globe for his care and rescue of elephants. When he died, thirty-one elephants walked over twelve miles to his South African house. They stood in reverential silence in a two day vigil outside his house without eating. My dog Darcy teaches me wisdoms about the role of animals and creatures in human life.

One in gender

Earlier in the book, there was a brief analysis of the origins of patriarchy in cultures and religions. The dismantling of patriarchy is a mammoth challenge for those who aspire to promote gender equity. Cultural norms about the subordination of women and taboos from menstruation are so deeply imbedded in tribal, religious and ethnic groups that one may well consider the task of equity almost impossible to attain. However, an encouraging sign is the rising levels of gender inclusion awareness and implementation of legislation in Western countries during the 20th century to ensure gender equity.

During the 20th century, gender voting rights were enshrined in law in Western orientated countries and the movement for pay equity is slowly being achieved. Women make career choices although the difficulty of reconciling parent responsibilities still often resides with the woman. The official church tends to emphasise the role of motherhood and family life for women rather than the individual rights of a woman. In very recent times, official statements about women by the church reflect a kind of romantic feminism (e.g. *Mulieris Dignitatem* 1988).

Except for the Catholic and Orthodox churches, most Christian churches have opened all levels of ministry to women. Misogynistic attitudes towards women have a long enduring history whose genesis resides in cultural biology and, for Christianity, in Greek philosophy. To illustrate how formidable is the task facing those advocating gender equity in Church life and ministry, consider these statements from eminent Christians:

St John Chrysostom (345-407), *A wife has just one purpose: to guard the possessions we have accumulated... God maintained the order of each sex by dividing the business of human life into two parts and assigned the more necessary and beneficial aspects to the man and the less important, inferior matters to the woman* (The kind of women who ought to be taken as wives, 4).

St Augustine, *I cannot think of any reason for woman's being made as man's helper, if we dismiss the reason of procreation* (Literal Commentary on Genesis 9:5).

St Thomas Aquinas, *As regards the individual nature, woman is defective and misbegotten, for the active power of the male seed tends to the production of a perfect likeness in the masculine sex; while the production of a woman comes from defect in the active power...* (Summa Theologica Q92, art 1 Reply Obj.1(25).

Martin Luther, *He rules the home and the state, wages war, defends his possessions, tills the soil, plants etc. The wife, on the other hand, is like a nail driven into the wall. She sits at home.* (Commentary on Tim 3:16).

Misogynist attitudes persist in contemporary culture. Note how only several decades ago *The Catholic Weekly*, the official newspaper of the archdiocese of Sydney, could write, *A young woman becoming a wife should think of her new state, not as one that is to make her happy but as one in which she is to make her husband happy. Her own happiness will be a by-product of that determination... The good wife realises that in becoming a wife she contracts to forget self and put her husband's happiness above her own wishes and desires* (26 February 1953). To be fair to the newspaper, it was only echoing the subjugation of wife theme in the encyclical of Pius XI (*Casti Connubii* 1930) and Pius XII's *Address to Married Couples* 1940). In recent years, Pope Paul VI and Pope John Paul II have written in support of the equality of women in society.

Although women have had minimal participation in the higher echelons of church structures, women have played a major part in Christian history. Mention has already been made of the prominent role in the ministry of Jesus and early church life. Mary the mother of Jesus is with Jesus in his ministry, even to the bitter end on Calvary (John 19). Mary Magdalene was given the title of *Apostle to the Apostles* in the early church. Junia was 'outstanding among the Apostles' (Romans 16:7), Phoebe was a 'deacon' and 'leader' of the Church in Cenchreae (Romans 16:1-2). Priscilla was a travelling missionary like Paul (Acts 18:2,19), women were prophets (Acts 21:9), women were leaders of House Churches (Nympha Colossians 4:15). Women are explicitly mentioned as deacons (1 Timothy 3:11).

In the New Testament writings, there is no indication of the criteria of who presided over the Eucharistic meal. Certainly there was no ritual called 'ordination' in the New Testament. The Twelve represented the Twelve tribes of the New Israel. There is nothing in New Testament literature about Jesus or the apostles instituting a regular process for ordination (Bokenkotter: 262).

It seems that whoever was leader of the household was the presider of the Eucharist (c.f. Schillebeeckx). Women were leaders or co-leaders in early Christian communities (e.g. Phoebe).

Until the Middle Ages, ordination (*ordo*) meant election by instillation of a person to perform a particular function in the Christian community. In the first thousand years, women could and sometimes did lead the Eucharist assembly (e.g. fifth century, Martia (*presbyteria*) at Poitiers). The majority of the members of the Pontifical Commission in 1976 concluded that the New Testament by itself alone does not settle the problem of the 'possible accession of women to the presbyterate'.

During the twelfth and thirteenth centuries, the whole notion of ordination experienced a dramatic change. The focus of power for ordination shifted from the community to the individual. The leader of the community was given the power himself to consecrate bread and wine. The rite of ordination gave him that individual power, divorced from the community. Those promoting ordination of women face the dilemma of advocating a return to the first 1000 years of an understanding of ordination or accepting the medieval theology of ordination during the second 1000 years of church history and working with it. With a rising percentage of Christian communities now no longer have regular Eucharist, something urgently needs to be done to rectify a serious issue of many Christians with no opportunity for regular Eucharist. Every Christian community has the right to have Eucharist.

Throughout the centuries, there is a long list of eminent women in church life. Women such as Teresa of Avila, the founders of Religious Congregations, Hildegard of Bingen, Mechtild of Magdeburg, Julian of Norwich, Elizabeth Fry, Mary Ward, Helen Keller, Elizabeth Seton, Mary MacKillop, Mother Teresa, Caroline Chisholm and Dorothy Day would be just a random sample of some women leaders in history. Women deacons were very important in the church during the first four centuries. The immersion of women in baptismal waters was conducted by women since the people to be baptised went into the water naked. Early Christian writers were quite explicit about the role of women deacons. Even as late as 1017, Pope Benedict VIII authorised the ordaining of deaconesses in Portugal. In the light of the role of women as deacons in early Christianity, it is a cause for reflection to note that the official church has currently closed off the option of women deacons. When the permanent deaconate was restored after the Second Vatican Council, the diaconate was for men only, a practice not in accord with early Christian traditions.

A patriarchal culture in church life will not be transformed by legislation only but by the recovery of the intuitive and feminine mind within the hearts of church leaders and the faithful generally. A male/female power struggle leads to a divisive church. A patriarchal church structure is an issue in the realm of pathology rather than theology.

The challenge of dismantling an entrenched patriarchal church culture is much more significant than concerns about who presides at the Eucharist or the prospect of female bishops. If the church is to give witness to the inclusive nature of God who is beyond gender, then its structures must give evidence of its commitment to inclusion. After all, Jesus went to his death to uphold the value of inclusion. Throughout the world, women are now in leadership roles of politics, military, industry and every facet of society. Why would we continue to believe that God has decided an exception of non-inclusion of women for church life? Cultural historians have explained the historical and biological rationale for patriarchy in past times. It is time now for the Christian community to move beyond practices and traditions about women that were based on defective genetics.

Women as a social group are the single most oppressed group in the world today. Rape, sex trafficking, domestic violence, genital mutilation, forced marriages, honour killing are just some of the manifestations of violence inflicted upon women. The World Health Organisation found that domestic and sexual violence affects thirty to sixty per cent of women in most countries. In South Africa every four seconds a woman is raped. Thirty per cent of men in South Africa admitted that they had raped a woman. In some countries doctors attending rape victims advise the raped women not to go to the police lest they be raped again. According to the National Crime Record Bureau in India the country recorded 24,206 rape cases in 2011. Conviction rates were only about 27% of the 75,000 molestation and sexual harassment incidents (United Nations Population Fund Executive Director). In China and other countries, girls are killed, aborted and abandoned simply because they are girls. What a powerful witness to social inclusion and justice would Christian churches give to the whole world if their structures and culture reflected a comprehensive gender inclusion? Christian communities provide extensive services to girls and women all over the world. Now is the time to take a more radical step of witness of full inclusion of women in every level of church life.

Inter-faith consciousness

One of the salient features of contemporary society since World War Two is the spread of diverse religious faiths across the globe. A visit to any shopping mall in major cities reveals multi-faith robes, prayer shawls, saffron robes, turbans, head scarves and multicoloured faces. In cities and towns, pagodas, temples and mosques now stand side by side with churches. Displaced populations, people suffering deprivation and persecution as well as migration have dispersed religions from specific geographical areas. Global technologies have expanded religious awareness and consciousness of the richness of religious traditions. International travel has facilitated people's direct experiences with religious traditions other than their own.

It would seem that human beings are becoming more aware of the long evolutionary journey of the divine presence in creation. There is a growing awareness that the 2000 year old story of any one faith such as Christianity is situated within the thousands of years old story of humans seeking to know and celebrate the Universal Spirit of the universe. There have been many revelations of the divine presence to humans, one of which is Christianity. For a Christian, the revelation of God through Jesus as Christ is a unique manifestation of God.

The Genesis origin myth symbolises the beginning of this great evolutionary quest for knowing something of the mystery of human relations with spiritual powers. There are no simple categories to capture the complexity of the character of revelation. How does one compare monotheistic religions (Judaism, Christianity, Islam) with Buddhism or Native American religions? Given the millions of people who subscribe to religious traditions with no definitive concept of God, only a hardy soul would dismiss these traditions as not integral to God's revelation.

However, a word of caution is a useful corrective to any illusion of global harmony between faiths. Although inter-faith relations have flourished during the last few decades, there are still serious tensions and sometimes violent clashes between religious groups. The conflicts are often a toxic mix of religion, ideologies economics, politics and envy. It is estimated that about 200 million Christians currently face serious threats, many more being persecuted than any other religious group. The great majority of Christians in the Middle East, the cradle of Christianity, has been driven into exile from their home lands.

Interfaith dialogue and understanding will be a hallmark of the Christian community's commitment to promote harmony for all people and the health of the planet. Adherents of different faiths are beginning to recognise that a healthy global world demands a complete and radical break with religious sectarianism and fundamentalism. A culture of religious pluralism does not subvert one's religious beliefs but situates the beliefs within an appreciation of how God's revelation has been manifest to different cultures and beliefs. In partnership with other religious traditions, Christians are enjoined to confront aggressive secularism, moral relativism and promote a society infused with spiritual values, especially values for justice.

Evolutionary ecclesial structures

All the research evidence in Western countries points to a serious crisis in Catholicism and also in all Christian faiths. In USA, one in every three people brought up Catholics are no longer Catholics. The second largest 'denomination' in USA is former Catholics. During the last twelve years there has been a decline of 10% in Catholic affiliation in the largest Catholic country, Brazil. Similar statistics in other Western countries would underline the serious nature of the crisis. Reasons for this crisis are beyond the scope of the book to discuss.

The basic issue in an evolutionary appreciation of the nature of the church is clarifying who or what is the church?

That church is a community of people gathered together in beliefs about God's revelation in Jesus and the Spirit to promote 'life in abundance' for all peoples on the earth and the wellbeing of creation. The church is not an elite self-enclosed tribal group committed to upholding a version of doctrinal purity. The very word 'Catholic' from the Greek *kata holikos* meaning 'making all things whole', is largely ignored in the current climate of the church which is intent in drawing all kinds of boundaries to designate who is 'in' and who is 'out'. For example, divorced and remarried Catholics are 'out' by not being permitted to receive communion in the Eucharist. Those who don't pay a church tax in Germany are 'out'. People of homosexual life orientation are designated as having an 'intrinsic disorder'. A fortress church spends energy on securing its walls against perceived enemies rather than being more proactive in reaching out to transform society with inclusive values.

There are three essential elements in the mission of the church and all three elements have to work together for the gospel. The three elements in the mission are as follows: scholars and theologians, the *sensus fidelium* or 'lived experience of the faithful' and the *magisterium* or official teaching church. To all intents and purposes, the first two elements, the work of theologians and the lived experience of the faithful, have been now marginalised or even discarded in practice by the *magisterium*. There is a depressing long list of theologians who have been silenced, censured and excluded for asking legitimate questions about the life of the Church. In the structures of the church there are no effective avenues for the voices of the laity to be heard. Even at ground level, opinions of the laity at synod gatherings are carefully filtered to remove any opinions contrary to official church positions on topics such as priestly celibacy, the status of women in church, women deacons and so on.

Today, the term *magisterium* refers exclusively to the teaching office of the bishops in communion with the Pope. However, since the time of Pope Pius XII (1939-1958) the scope of the term *magisterium* has been even further restricted to the Pope and the Curia in doctrinal teachings. Such a confining role of the *magisterium* is not supported by historical traditions concerning the exercise of doctrinal teaching authority. In the first 1000 years, the bishops drew from the faith life of the whole people of God in their teachings. Many bishops in the early church were theologians. During the second millennium, theologians became more removed from the teaching authority of bishops. A further development, especially in the late nineteenth century, was the growing use of the 'encyclical' by popes to exercise papal teaching authority.

The *magisterium* does not possess all truth. Its role is to proclaim truth that is distilled from the wisdoms of the whole People of God guided by the Holy Spirit. The days of the famous ancient saying, *Roma locuta est, causa finita est* (Latin: 'Rome has spoken, the matter has ended') reflects a church imperial culture. An imperial church culture becomes obsolete with the recovery of the baptismal right of every Christian not just to **belong** to the church but to **be** the church. The post-Vatican Two teachings on what baptism means assumes a movement from lay dependency in a hierarchical culture to an empowerment of all the People of God for discipleship. The Vatican Two document *Dei Verbum*, the Dogmatic Constitution on Divine Revelation, taught that the word of God was given to the whole church, not just to the bishops (n 10). The *magisterium* is a servant to the word of God and is not superior to it.

The fourth century was a turning point in the history of the church. In retrospect, one might suggest that what happened was a retrograde step in a holistic ecclesiology. Under the Emperor Constantine (313), Christianity was freed from persecution. Within a short time, Christianity became the official religion of the Empire. With the collapse of the Empire in the West, the church became the political as well as ecclesial rock to provide order and organisation for a society in disarray. The Roman Empire was being invaded by marauding tribes from the East. Gradually, church structures mirrored the Imperial model of government in the Empire. The Imperial model of church became its 'modus operandi' as a top-downwards structure with the bishops and clergy on top and the laity at the bottom.

Hierarchy and priesthood are unknown concepts in the New Testament churches. However, by the time of St Ignatius of Antioch (d c 107), the threefold division of ministries of elders (*presbyteroi*), deacons (*diakonoi*) and overseers (*episcopoi*) were beginning to become more widespread in church life. About 200 years after the death of Jesus ,we began to hear of the distinction between clergy (*ordo*) and laity (Tertullian 155-220), at least in the sense of how this distinction is understood today. From the gospel model of community of disciples, the church had been transformed into a dichotomy of clergy possessing the spiritual power and the laity as 'followers'.

In an increasingly bureaucratic world, the ever present danger for such a large institution as the Christian church is for 'churchianity' to replace Christianity. Richard Rohr's comment about the nature of the church is insightful in today's ecclesial climate. He suggests that the early church inherited the Exodus tradition of setting people free. Certainly this theme of freedom characterised the mission of Jesus (Luke 4:17). However, by the time of the fourth century, the church gradually tended to move away from the freedom tradition and reverted to the 'priestly' tradition of Leviticus and Numbers where laws and structures became an overriding concern in church governance.

The notion of authority within an imperial model of church assumes that someone at the apex of the ecclesial pyramid sends down directives and those below in the hierarchal order simply do what they are told. An exercise of authority itself does not make something correct. There are numerous examples from church history where proclamations by popes have been reversed in succeeding generations of Christians e.g. Pope Boniface VIII's papal bull *Unam Sanctum* (1302) claimed papal sovereignty over both the sacred and temporal realms . The Second Vatican Council's Dogmatic Constitution on the church declared the opposite to that statement by Boniface. All exercises of authority in the church have to be tested for authenticity against the values of the gospel.

After the French revolution (1789) and the spread of democracy in the last two hundred years among many Western countries, the imperial model of the church no longer has credence in the Western world. An imperial model of Church is clearly dysfunctional as a model of governance as well as being defective ecclesiology. The imperial model of church disempowers the laity and the local church. A governing church must exhibit accountability and transparency to the whole People of God. The tragedy of the clergy abuse situation has more than demonstrated the urgency for transparency as well as compassion. A rising tide of voices in many countries is insisting that the church return to its origins as a community of disciples who listen and share wisdoms. The hierarchy is integral of the church's structure but it must exercise authority in concert with the other two elements of the Christian community, the scholars and the lived experience of the faithful.

The word 'authority' is linked with the Latin *augere* meaning 'to make bigger'. Christian authority is best exercised when, in the spirit of servant leadership

(Mark 10:42), it makes more expansive the Good News of the reign of God and 'life in abundance'. Christian leadership must be conducted in a prayerful mode, sharing with informed people, research and above all, discernment of the Spirit. The current inflexible rigidity of some aspects of Church leadership is beginning to push the Catholic Church towards a deeply divided church or even schism. The movement towards a divided church will only be reversed when church leaders humbly listen carefully to the voices of the Spirit and discern as a whole People of God how best the Christ story might be told and lived in today's world.

Dialogue is a two-way street. There is something of a paradox in a church that insists on religious freedom in the secular world but punishes dissenting voices within its membership by an enforced consensus. Possibly the greatest obstacle to the new evangelisation movement is not secularism or moral relativism, but the unwillingness of the highest echelons of church leadership to read 'the signs of the times', listen, research, utilise the gifts of members and be prepared to change or modify those church structures that inhibit the proclamation of the gospel.

The power structures in the church have not yet grasped this basic principle of governance. Acts 15 offers a helpful model for how church leadership should make decisions. At the Council of Jerusalem (49 CE), early Christians were faced with a critical decision about whether or not new followers of Jesus had to follow the law of Moses and be circumcised. Speakers for and against the proposal discussed the issue. After hearing both sides, a decision was finally made to, *not to trouble those Gentiles who are turning to God (19)* by imposing the law of Moses on them.

Religious cultural wars do nothing to promote the Kingdom. Cultural theological rock throwing diverts energy of the Spirit into useless conflict that diminishes a celebration of God's expansive love. Passivity, bitterness and cynicism are corrosive fruits of a polarised church.

The church is not a European institution. Much of the vitality of the church now happens in Asia and Africa and these churches scarcely register on the church's central governing radar. As a verification of the previous observation, note the geographical composition and status of key people in the Curia. They are predominately European clergy and almost completely unrepresentative of the global church. The laity, especially lay women, are virtually absent from any senior position in central church governance. It is little wonder that the comings and goings of the governing church have such little impact on ordinary Catholics in Western countries. If people are not listened to, they no longer listen. If Baptism is a sacrament of initiation into the Christian community, then it is a baptismal right of every Christian to have some say in the life of the Christian community. The New Testament makes it very clear that Jesus removed a class system from religion.

The election of Pope Francis I in 2013 is perhaps the beginning the shift to a world-centred church rather than a European centred church, at least in governance.

The disenfranchising of the People of God from any real investment in matters that pertain to their actual Christian life is poignantly illustrated by the advent of the new revised liturgy in 2011. The representatives of the Bishops in English speaking countries (ICEL) had worked tirelessly in their preparation for a revised liturgy. Quite unexpectedly, in 2002, ICEL's almost completed revision of the liturgy was discarded and another non representative central structure (*Vox Clara*) was constituted to produce a new liturgy based on a literal translation of the Latin without its obvious concerns of using language conducive to worship and gender inclusion.

The Genesis Origin myth describes the beginning of this long evolutionary journey with all its ebbs and flows. Our present era is one of rapid change. The eminent theologian Karl Rahner (d 2010) once said, 'The future Christian will be a mystic or nothing' (actually Panikkar had said this prediction thirty years before Rahner). I believe his remark is very appropriate for a Christian today who is called to the heart of God's revelation as mystics do. Mystics are fond of saying, 'learning to rest in God'. Living with paradox, contradictions, ambivalence is not easy, especially for those who prize religious security and clear parameters of belief. For a Christian, the heart of God's revelation is in Jesus who became the Christ through the energy of the Spirit. To cling to a revelation that is paradoxical, a believer will struggle in faith to live with the mystery of the light and dark side of God. The whole Pascal mystery is a paradox where the crucified One becomes the resurrected One.

Logic does not fare well in living the Christian story. The Bible is really a subversive illogical book. The social and religious 'outsiders' such as Samaritans, tax collectors, women and shepherds, become 'insiders'. Jesus turned his world upside down as to who was who in God's sight. The science of Emergence reminds us that new structures in the church may suddenly appear from previous dissipative elements in previous forms of church life. Who knows if and when the Spirit will move the Christian community to experience radical change within an evolving world?

Liturgy and worship

If we look at the interpretation of the Genesis origin myth as a symbolic story about the beginning of the evolutionary journey of humankind rather than

Fall, some liturgical prayers may need review or at least be open to other symbolic interpretations. An example of one such prayer is the much loved liturgical text, the *Exsultet*, sung on Holy Saturday night. Its verses reflect the Fall tradition:

> *It is truly right that with full hearts and minds and voices,*
> *We should praise the unseen God, the all-powerful Father*
> *and his only Son our Lord Jesus Christ*
> *For Christ has ransomed us with his blood and paid for us the price of*
> *Adam's sin*
> *to the eternal Father.*
> *O happy fault, a necessary sin of Adam which gained for us so great*
> *a redeemer.*

There is no ready pastoral response to the dilemma of reviewing many liturgical prayers which reflect the Fall/redemption themes of the New Testament. By raising an awareness of the theme of Emergence rather than Fall in the Genesis origin myth, liturgical prayers may be interpreted at a symbolic rather than literal level. There would be theological and liturgical mayhem if radical decisions were taken to minimise or eliminate all prayers emanating out of a Fall tradition.

Hope

Christian hope is not some kind of naive expectation that everything will be okay simply because God loves us. Hope emerges in faith through the struggles with pain and despair as well as with the blessings of life. The church in Western countries is now entering a 'dark night of the soul' at the level of declining influence in the public arena and a growing disenchantment with how church life is conducted. However, at another level, people are participating in liturgy, promoting justice and earth care, proactive citizenship, loving and caring in family and single life. Hope is grounded in faith that the God of love will grace the mystery of paradox, the dilemmas and the ongoing quest to be faithful to the gospel. I cannot think of a better statement on hope than the words of St Augustine, 'Hope has two beautiful daughters; their names are Anger and Courage. Anger that things are the way they are. Courage to make them the way they ought to be'.

A Christ-centred church must be a truthful church. Charles Taylor in his writings describes this era as an 'Age of Authenticity' where there is an imperative to foster a congruence between what is said and what is done.

Conclusion

This chapter has considered the person of Jesus as the Christ and the journey of the Christian community. If the Genesis origin story is interpreted not as Fall but rather a story of the birth of human consciousness, then we need to review our understanding of the mission of Jesus. The primary motive for the incarnation was not to rectify a purported moral failure in past history but to fuse into oneness humanity and divinity (deification) within an evolutionary world.

During the last 2000 years, the Christian community has lived and told the Christ story across the globe. If the context of the story is set in the dynamism of an evolutionary faith journey, the Christian community will be open to flexibility in its governance structures, ministry, evangelisation, inculturation, liturgy and worship, devotions and creative approaches to enhance 'life in abundance' to all people and creation. The current buzz word 'continuity' in Catholic circles should mean above all, continuity with, and fidelity to, God's revelation through Jesus and the Spirit rather than time and cultural bound proclamations of dogma. The Christian will work cooperatively with all religious traditions and public services to realise more fully God's dream for a harmonious and just world.

CHAPTER EIGHT

Conclusion

In the final chapter, I wish to draw together the various themes in the book.

One of the most significant issues facing religious traditions in the modern world is to forge a creative partnership with modern science for the wellbeing of all things in creation. Scientific consciousness impacts almost every feature of contemporary life in the Western world. In particular, evolutionary science challenges religious traditions to review how their time-honoured beliefs are expressed.

The science of evolution has been one of the most far reaching scientific discoveries during the last one hundred and fifty years, affecting not only science itself but such areas as cultural change, religions, spirituality, theology, technology, social sciences and cosmology. The inner world of evolutionary consciousness is as significant as the outer world of scientific advances. An evolutionary world view has the potential to bring many benefits to the whole of the earth community if people are seriously motivated to address current and future global concerns. Although religion and science have different assumptions about reality and methodology, religious beliefs should not contradict proven science.

How might the Christian story be told within an evolutionary perspective?

For Christians, the incarnation is a central event, fusing humanity and divinity with the advent of Jesus who became the Christ. The evolutionary story of *homo sapiens* narrates how humans emerged over millions of years out of primitive life forms. Humanity is firmly placed **within** the process of evolution. The human species has evolved out of stardust. If contemporary Christians insist in taking seriously the incarnation, then they are encouraged to draw from the insights of evolution in telling the Christian story. Because humans are within the evolving process of creation, they possess the power to shape the future for the betterment of all things in creation.

Our expanding universe is about 13.7 billion years old and our solar system was born about 4.8 billion years ago. In an awesome moment of the beginning of creation, the Big Bang exploded with a flash of light and generation of matter. Out of almost nothing came everything that we are and have in the universe. Some primal form of humans appeared about two million years ago although *homo sapiens* is perhaps only 120,000 old. Studies on the evolution of the human species propose that there were two, or possibly even other strands of human species which eventually became the one genetic strand of the human species which we have today. Symbolic consciousness, self reflection and the power to make moral choices became integral to the essential nature of *homo sapiens*. About 100,000 to 80,000 years ago, a small group of humans left North-Eastern Africa and spread across the globe.

The power of symbolic consciousness enabled humans to express their experiences in art, music and story. Tribal groups composed communal stories to articulate their desire to explain the mysteries of life around them and their origins. Their origin myths were composed and passed on to later generations as an explanation of the meaning of the world around them. One such myth was composed by the Hebrew people to explain the paradox of the goodness of God in creation and the prevalence of evil and chaos in nature. The first three chapters of Genesis describe this mysterious ambivalence in symbolic language. When the symbolism of the origin myth was later lost in a literal interpretation as a framework for the Christian story, a credibility gap widened between the literalism of the Fall story and the insights of evolutionary science.

Studies on the evolution of the human species are in general agreement that there was no one couple Adam and Eve who began the whole generation of the human race. Sin did not enter the human condition by some single moral failing by Adam and Eve. It is the nature of humans to make moral choices for good or evil. The Genesis origin myth describes how humans have the freedom to choose or reject God's providential care.

Death was not a punishment for sin. The image of a world without death cannot be scientifically envisaged. All things die in an evolutionary understanding of the universe. Literal interpretations of the origin myth left a series of complex theological dilemmas in the telling of the Christian story, not the least of which is how the mission of Jesus has been understood in Christian history and also the nature of the human person.

The Genesis origin myth has traditionally been interpreted in Christian theology as a Fall. Sin and disorder were explained in this myth as a failure by Adam and Eve to obey God's command. In the New Testament, the interpretation of the myth as a Fall was a traditional context for understanding the mission of Jesus, especially his crucifixion and death. Given the 2000 year old formidable corpus of redemption theology as a dominant theme in Christology, the interpretation of the myth as Fall will perhaps always be a traditionally accepted lens to situate the Christian narrative.

However, in the light of evolutionary science, this book explores an alternative interpretation of the origin myth and its implications for the Christian story.

The alternative interpretation of Emergence not Fall intends both to preserve the core of the Christian message and better align the Christian narrative with the insights of modern science, especially evolution.

If we interpret the Genesis origin myth as the Emergence of the human species on the great journey of enlightenment, then there is another interpretation of the mission of Jesus who became the Christ. For Christians, the incarnation came to exemplify the meaning of the bringing together of divinity and humanity in a unique way through Jesus as Christ. His ministry of preaching and teaching proclaimed a God of graciousness and liberation.

The theme of 'life in abundance' (John 10:10) sums up the mission of Jesus to reveal and witness to a God of life. His redemptive sufferings and death were the consequence of his utter fidelity to his mission to set oppressed people free. The resurrection of Jesus as the Christ removed the meaningless of death. The resurrection of Jesus is a prototype for the transformation of each person to another phase of a glorified life. The mission of Jesus was not a backward looking event to restore a purported breakdown of relationships which happened in a bygone age, but a forward looking experience of who we might become. For Christians, Christ as redeemer and saviour is bringing humans and creation into wholeness. Christology has to be rescued from the literalism of the Genesis origin myth of the Fall.

For a Christian, the life journey is not so much about a restoration of something that went wrong in distant past times, but a journey towards a deification within an evolutionary celebration of the universe.

The doctrine of original sin, which was born out the interpretation of the Fall tradition, extended the inherited sin of the world to each individual person. Such a sinful birthmark left an indelible pessimistic character on Christian anthropology and spirituality. In an evolutionary perspective on humankind, people are born into original grace with a propensity to choose good and evil in their very nature. Over many thousands of years in the social evolution of the human species, people learned to make moral choices for good or evil. There was no one morally sinful act in our evolutionary past. There was no primal defiance of a divine power which condemned all humanity to a sinful heritage.

The Genesis origin myth may be interpreted as a story of how a static stage of consciousness dissolved when almost humans crossed the threshold into self-consciousness and began their great evolutionary journey of consciousness and enlightenment. To take the fruit of the Tree of Knowledge was the decisive step in crossing the threshold into self-consciousness. From the very beginning, humans have been in an unending quest to understand the mysteries of life and reverence the presence of the Universal Spirit. About four thousand years ago, great religions began to emerge. There have been many divine revelations in human history, all of which offer different wisdoms for social groups to relate to others and the cosmos.

At a particular time and place on this evolutionary journey, Christians believe that the Divine Spirit revealed God's presence in Jesus who became the Christ. The Christian community, in partnership with the great religious traditions and indigenous spiritualities, is enjoined to enhance the lives of people and contribute to planetary health. The cosmic journey of life which began billions of years ago, continues as an ongoing evolutionary journey of change and possibilities. There are momentous social issues to be addressed today towards planetary health. Because humans have emerged within the process of evolution, they have the responsibility and power to make choices for the future good in unchartered territories.

As explained earlier in the book, at first sight the theme of this book may appear to have little relevance to the day-to-day struggles of people such as coping with caring for children, engaging in relationships, working, paying bills, poverty, recreation, natural disasters, family life, retirement, issues of justice and earth care, refugees and so on.

However, a closer look at the theme brings the topic right back into ordinary Christian life with such questions as:

- *Do people have an origin myth that gives meaning and direction to their lives?*

- *What does it mean for a person to live harmoniously in the network of life in creation?*

- *Who is Jesus and what does he mean for people in today's world?*

- *In partnership with the great religious traditions, what significant contributions can Christianity bring to spiritual values and justice in the world?*

- *Where do the Christian story and evolutionary science meet in their quest for truth?*

- *How might science and religion work together to create a better world?*

- *How might a Christian anthropology offer society a positive view of human nature?*

- *How might evil, sin and suffering be explained?*

An emerging Christianity acknowledges and celebrates its 2000 year old formidable heritage of spiritual wisdoms, works for justice, liturgy, arts, cathedrals, music, heroic women and men and centuries of care for the disadvantaged.

Nevertheless, the church cannot not live on memories alone. The   power of Spirit imagination will envisage what might be for 'life in abundance' in creation. We are at a threshold point in history where there is a birthing of a new consciousness that will not be reversed. Our understanding of God situates the Divine Energy **within** the evolutionary process of creation, not **outside** its dynamics of change. Christianity, like all religions, is faced with the prospect of grounding their traditions within an evolutionary worldview. The temptation for religions is to lose courage and abandon the pilgrimage of faith by dropping anchor in safe harbours of a past theological refuge.

Is the Christian church prepared to make a prophetic step and seize the moment for renewal? The Chinese word 'crisis' means 'an opportunity to do something different'. The decline in affiliation of Christians and polarisation in the church in the Western world have the potential to be a catalyst for revitalisation or a timid option of settling down as members of an irrelevant sect.

There is no doubt that the formulation of the Christian story is being challenged to develop a new theological paradigm which is founded on an evolutionary perspective of creation including the evolution of the human person. Sooner or later, this challenge of developing a new *Summa* will have to be officially addressed. Given the rapidity of cultural change, sooner rather than later is a preferred option for the vitality and relevance of the Christian faith.

What are some salient features which would embody this revitalisation?

I would propose the following features:

- Celebrate the diverse divine revelations in the history of humankind.

- Embrace the possibilities of *becoming* in an evolutionary perspective on the Christian story.

- Foster an inclusive spirituality which helps people find deep meaning in their lives.

- Work with all religious traditions and public agencies for the justice and wellbeing of creation.

- Honour the wisdoms and traditions of all religions.

- For Christians, celebrate and share the rich heritage of the Christian story.

- Deepen opportunities for encountering God in Christ and through the Spirit.

- Engage in renewal of the Christian community whose spirit and culture faithfully reflect the mission of Jesus the Christ.

- Review the ministries and structures of the church in the light of their effectiveness in facilitating the mission of the church.

An enlarged vision of Christianity in its evolutionary faith journey will embrace the best features of its heritage in this unfolding global era of consciousness. Faith is not about securing certainty in probing the mystery of God. Faith is a groping forward, trusting in God's goodness and living with the ambivalence of believing. In our world now, which may be described as an epoch of post optimism, the medieval theologians teach us about a basic belief in God's care and their faith perspective on life where, according to these theologians, *bonum est diffusivum sui* (Latin: 'goodness spreads itself out everywhere').

In the first chapters of the Bible, we read about a Tree of Life and a Tree of Knowledge, a tree of knowing how to make moral choices. In the final book of the Bible, the Book of Revelation, we read again about the Tree of Life. The Tree of Life in the book of Revelation is a tree for healing, *and the leaves of the tree are for the healing of nations... and there will be no more night; they need no light of lamp or sun, for the Lord God will be their light, and they will reign forever and ever* (Revelations 22:2,5). To choose *life in abundance* from the Tree of Knowledge is to choose an Emergence into the blessings of the Tree of Life.

> *Make me know your ways, O Lord;*
> *Teach me your paths.*
> *Lead me in your truth and teach me* (Psalm 25:4-5).

RESOURCES

The resources listed below have been helpful in writing this book. Internet sites have been invaluable as resources.

Armstrong, K. *A History of God: From Abraham to the Present: the 4000-year Quest for God.* Random House, London. Vintage, 1999.

Armstrong, K. *The Battle for God: A History of Fundamentalism.* New York. The Random House Publishing Group, 2000.

Armstrong, K. *Twelve Steps to a Compassionate Life.* London. The Bodley Head, 2011.

Berry, T. *The Dream of the Earth.* San Francisco. Sierra Club Books, 1988.

Bourke, V.J. (ed.). *The Essential Augustine.* New York. Mentor-Omega Books. 1964.

Bokenkotter, K. 'Holy Orders: The Meaning of Ministry Today' in *Dynamic Catholicism: A Historical Catechism.* New York. Image Books. 1992.

Boyle, E.M.OP. *Science as Sacred Metaphor: An Evolving Revelation.* Collegeville, Minnesota. Liturgical Press. 2006.

Cannato, J. *Field of Compassion: How the new Cosmology is Transforming Spiritual Life.* Notre Dame. Indiana. Sorin Books, 2010.

Catechism of the Catholic Church. (1994). Homebush NSW. St Pauls.

Cohen, A. *Evolutionary Enlightenment: A New Path to Spiritual Awakening.* New York. Select Books, Inc. 2011.

Delio, I. *Christ in Evolution.* Maryknoll, New York. Orbis Books, 2008.

Delio, I. *The Emergent Christ: Exploring the Meaning of Catholic in an Evolutionary Universe.* Maryknoll, New York. Orbis Books, 2011.

Edwards, D. *The God of Evolution: A* Trinitarian Theology. New York. Paulist Press, 1999.

Edwards, D. *Ecology at the Heart of Faith.* Maryknoll, New York. Orbis Books, 2006.

Edwards, D. *How God Acts: Creation, Redemption and Special Divine Action.* ATF Ltd. Hindmarsh. SA, 2010.

Edwards, D. *Jesus and the Natural World: Exploring a Christian Approach to Ecology.* Mulgrave. Vic. Garratt Publishing, 2012

Elmer, I. J. *Paul, Jerusalem and the Judaisers: The Galatian Crisis in the Broader Historical Context.* Fitzroy, Victoria, Australia. Australian Catholic University. Doctoral dissertation, 2007.

Flannery, T. *Here on Earth: An Argument for Hope.* Melbourne. The Text Publishing Company, 2010.

Fox, M. *Original Blessing: A Primer in Creation Theology.* Santa Fe, New Mexico. Bear and Company, 1983.

Freeman, C. *The Closing of the Western Mind: The Rise of Faith and the Fall of Reason.* Sydney. Random House Australia, 2002.

Hall, G.& Hendriks, J (eds). *Dreaming a new Earth: Ramon Panikkar and Indigenous Spiritualities.* Preston, Vic. Mosaic Press, 2012.

Hubbard, B. M. *Birth 2012 and Beyond: Humanity's Great Shift to the Age of Conscious Evolution.* Shift Books 2012.

Johnson, E. A. *Quest for the Living God: Mapping Frontiers in the Theology of God.* New York. Continuum, 2007.

Johnson, P. *A History of Christianity.* London. Wedenfeld and Nicholson. 1976.

Johnston SJ. W. (ed.). *The Cloud of Unknowing and the Book of Privy Counseling.* New York. Image Books Doubleday and Company. 1973.

Kirkwood, P. *The Quiet Revolution: The Emergence of Interfaith Consciousness.* Sydney. ABC Books, 2007.

Kung, H. *The Beginning of all Things: Science and Religion.* Cambridge, UK. William B. Eerdmans Publishing Company. Translated by John Bowden, 2007.

Kushner, H.S. *How Good do We have to Be? A new Understanding of Guilt and Forgiveness.* Boston. Little, Brown and Company, 1996.

McDonagh, S. *Fukushima: Death Knell for Nuclear Energy?* Dublin. The Columba Press. 2012.

MacGregor, D. *Blue Sky God: The Evolution of Science and Christianity.* UK. Circle Books, 2012.

Mahoney SJ, J. *Christianity in Evolution: An Exploration.* Georgetown University Press. Washington, USA, 2012.

Metz, J.B.(1981). *The Emergent Church: The Future of Christianity in a Postbourgeois World.* New York. Crossroad.

Morwood, M. *From Sand to Solid Ground: Questions of Faith for Modern Christians.* Richmond, Victoria. Spectrum Publications Pty. Ltd, 2007.

Nolan, A. *Jesus Today: A Spirituality of Radical Freedom.* Maryknoll, New York. Orbis Books, 2007.

Nowotny-Keane, E. *Amazing Encounters: Direct Communication from the Afterlife.* East Kew, Victoria. David Lovell Publishing, 2009.

Oliver, P. *World Faiths: An Introduction.* London. Hodder Education, 2001.

O'Murchu, D. *Quantum Theology: Spiritual Implications of the New Physics.* New York. The Crossroad Publishing Company, 1997.

O'Murchu, D. *Growing in Faith: Growing in Wisdom and Understanding.* Maryknoll. New York 10545. Orbis Books, 2010.

Pagola, J.A. *Jesus: An Historical Approximation.* Miami, Florida. Convivium Press, 2001.

Panikkar, R. *The Cosmotheandric Experience.* Maryknoll. New York. Orbis Books, 1993.

Phipps, C. *Evolutionaries: Unlocking the Spiritual and Cultural Potential of Science's Greatest Idea.* New York. Harper Perennial. 2012.

Regan, H. D. & Worthing, M. Wm(eds). *Interdisciplinary Perspectives and Biological Evolution.* Adelaide. Australian Theological Forum. 2002.

Robinson, G. *Confronting Power and Sex in the Catholic Church: Reclaiming the Spirit of Jesus.* Mulgrave, Victoria. John Garratt Publishing, 2007.

Sacks. J. *The Great Partnership: God, Science and the Search for Meaning.* London. Hodder & Stoughton, 2011.

Schillebeeckx, E. *Ministry: A Case for Change.* London. SCM Press, 1981.

Silk, J. *Horizons of Cosmology: Exploring the Worlds Seen and Unseen.* West Conshohocken, PA. Templeton Press. 2009.

Smith, A.B. *The God Shift: Our Changing Perception of the Ultimate Mystery.* London. New Millennium, 1996.

Smith, A.B. *A reason for Living and Hoping: A Christian Appreciation of the Emerging New Age of Consciousness.* London. St Paul Publications, 2002.

Smith, A.B. *God, Energy and the Field.* O Books. Winchester, UK, 2008.

Smith, P. R. *Integral Christianity: The Spirit's Call to Evolve*. St Paul, Minnesota. Paragon House, 2011.

Stewart, R.J. *The Elements of Creation Myths*. Longmead, Dorset. Element Books Limited, 1989.

Swimme, B. T. & Tucker M.E. *Journey of the Universe*. New Haven and London. Yale University Press, 2011.

Tacey, D. *The Spirituality Revolution: The Emergence of Contemporary Spirituality*. Sydney. HarperCollins Publishers, 2003.

Tarnas, R. *The Passion of the Western Mind: Understanding the Ideas that have shaped our World View*. New York. Ballantine Books, 1991.

Taylor, C. *A Secular Age*. Harvard. Mass. Harvard University Press, 2007.

Toews, J. E. *The story of original sin*. Eugene, Oregon. Pickwick Publications, 2013.

Treston, K. *A Modern Credo: Telling the Christ Story within the Context of Creation*. Mulgrave. Victoria. John Garratt Publishing, 2010.

Wessels OP C. *Jesus in the New Universe Story*. Maryknoll, New York. Orbis Books, 2003.

Wilber, K. *Integral Spirituality: A Startling new Role for Religion in the Modern and Post Modern World*. Boston and London. Integral Books, 2007.

Zohar, D. And Marshall, I. *SQ: Spiritual Intelligence: The Ultimate Intelligence*. London. Bloomsbury, 2000.

There is a host of DVDs on the topic. Four relevant DVDs which were used in the composition of the book are listed below:

Journey of the Universe. The Epic story of Cosmic, Earth and Human Transformation. InCA Productions.

Origins of Us. BBC.

How to Grow a Planet. BBC.

Charles Darwin and the Tree of Life. David Attenborough BBC.

GLOSSARY

Altruism: Human behaviour which is directed towards the wellbeing of others.

Aquinas OP (1225-1274): St Thomas Aquinas, a Dominican priest, is perhaps the most eminent philosopher and theologian in Christian history. His most famous works are *Summa Theologica* and *Summa Contra Gentiles*.

Atonement: The act of healing the breakdown of relationships between God and humankind.

Augustine (354-430): One of the influential theologians in Christianity. His vast writings in theology and philosophy have significantly shaped the Christian story with his teachings on original sin. His most famous works include *Confessions of St Augustine, City of God* and *On Christian Doctrine*.

Bohm, David (1917-1991): A prominent quantum physicist who described the changing nature of matter.

Charism: The inner spirit of a group that gives the group its foundational character.

Clericalism: A church culture which holds that the core work of the church is done by clergy with laity as helpers. Clericalism is not to be confused with the ministry of priesthood.

Cosmology: The study of the origins and evolution of the universe.

Darwin, Charles (1809-1881):an English naturalist whose research on evolution demonstrated that all species have descended over time from common ancestry. Neo-Darwinism further developed and refined Darwin's theories in the light of contemporary evolutionary science.

Dissipative structure: A new dynamic state which emerges through a process of transformation out of chaos.

Gnosticism: An early Christian heresy which denied the reality of the incarnation. Gnosticism stressed the role of inner knowledge and believed in the dualism of matter (bad) and soul (good).

Hermeneutics: A study of the principles which govern the interpretation of any text.

Hominids: Ape-like creatures, the species immediately preceding the advent of *homo sapiens*.

Inculturation: The process of adapting the gospel and church life to individual cultures.

Imperial model of church: A model of church emanating from the imperial model of governance in the Roman Empire. The imperial model of church was consolidated in the Middle Ages and functions as a top down structure of the Christian community with the laity on the lowest level of the structure.

Magisterium: The teaching authority of the church, held by the Pope and bishops.

Morphic resonance: The biologist Rupert Sheldrake proposed that an individual organism can be influenced by the behaviour of another organism of the same species without physical contact.

Myth: A sacred story which is not scientifically true but contains religious truth.

Neo-platonic philosophy: Ancient Greek philosophy (3rd-6th centuries) which taught that everything emanates in a hierarchical order from the One.

Omega point: Teilhard's concept of the apex of the human consciousness.

Paleoanthropologists: Those who study human origins.

Panentheism: A belief that God's presence infuses the whole of the universe. God's being, however, is greater than the universe.

Teilhard de Chardin (1881-1955): A distinguished geologist-palaeontologist and Jesuit priest whose works linked religious beliefs with evolutionary science.